FAVOURITE
POEMS

FAVOURITE POEMS

A selection of the world's best-loved verse

Compiled by Frances Evans
Illustrated by Madeleine David

ARCTURUS

We would like to thank the following people for permission to reproduce poems in this book: The Literary Trustees of Walter de la Mare and The Society of Authors as their representative *The Birthnight* (page 34) and *The Listeners* (page 135) by Walter de la Mare; Tom Cornford *Childhood* (54) by Frances Darwin Cornford; Alison Webster *On a Cat, Aging* (page 94) by Alexander Gray; Barbara Levy Agency *Everyone Sang* (page 176) by Siegfried Sassoon.

Front cover: *Cats in a Magnolia Tree*, Liz Wright/Bridgeman Images

ARCTURUS

This edition published in 2016 by Arcturus Publishing Limited
26/27 Bickels Yard, 151–153 Bermondsey Street,
London SE1 3HA

Text and design © Arcturus Holdings Limited
Illustrations © Madeleine David

ISBN: 978-1-78404-656-9
AD004425UK

Printed in China

 # Contents

CONTENTS

• • • • • • • • • • •

Love

CONTENTS

Animals and Nature

Magic, Fantasy and Nonsense

Travels and Place

Reflections and Musings

War and Peace

Mortality and Remembrance

Ballads and Folk Poems

Introduction

We do not know who composed the first poem, in what circumstances or on what subject. But however it began, poetry has been an important part of our human culture for thousands of years.

Firstly, there is poetry that 'speaks to our condition', poetry that can express love and loss, hope and despair, fear and anger – the whole gamut of human emotions – in words and images that most of us could never hope to articulate ourselves. You will find moving examples of such poetry in this book.

But of course, not all poetry is intended to trace the heights and depths of our human experience. There is more to life, and to poetry, than that. Some poems tell stories. Some poems paint pictures. Some poems lead us to see the world around us in new and unexpected ways. And some poems are written to make us laugh – at life, at other people, at ourselves. You will find examples of these, too, in this anthology of much-loved poetry.

Those of us who love poetry often have a favourite poem. It may be one that we learned at school, and that for some reason came to mean more to us than simply a subject for study; it may be a poem we learned at home, perhaps read to us at bedtime; it may be a poem we associate with a special event in our lives; it may be a poem we simply came across by chance. For whatever reason, it is a poem we love and treasure. This is a collection of just such poems.

For convenience, the poems have been gathered together by topic, such as 'Animal and Nature Poems', 'Travels and Place', 'War and Peace' and, of course, 'Love'. And while the majority of poets included are from the British Isles – Shakespeare, Wordsworth, Tennyson, Keats, Kipling, Coleridge, Burns, Scott and Yeats among others – poets and poetry from other parts of the English-speaking world have not been neglected: you will find here, for example, from North America Dickinson, Gilman, Thoreau and Whitman, Service and McCrae, and from Australia the famous Banjo Paterson, author of 'Waltzing Matilda'.

Like 'Waltzing Matilda' and Robert Burns's 'Red, Red Rose', some of the poems included in this collection are perhaps better known as songs to be sung than as poems to be recited, but they are well worthy of inclusion in a poetry anthology.

Of course, it may be that your own favourite poem is not included here. Indeed, you may not have a favourite poem at all. In either case, read and enjoy this collection of other people's favourites. By the time you reach the end of the book, you may have found one, too.

Lastly, do not read this book too quickly – like fine wines, poems should be savoured. And if you do find a favourite among these poems, why not memorize it? A poem is a companion for life, especially if it is one you carry with you in your head as well as your heart.

George Davidson

Children, Family and Home

'Come, my little children, here are songs for you'

Come, my little children, here are songs for you;
Some are short and some are long, and all, all are new.
You must learn to sing them very small and clear,
Very true to time and tune and pleasing to the ear.

Mark the note that rises, mark the notes that fall,
Mark the time when broken, and the swing of it all.
So when night is come, and you have gone to bed,
All the songs you love to sing shall echo in your head.

Robert Louis Stevenson

Infant Joy

I have no name
I am but two days old.—
What shall I call thee?
I happy am
Joy is my name,—
Sweet joy befall thee!

Pretty joy!
Sweet joy but two days old,
Sweet joy I call thee;
Thou dost smile.
I sing the while
Sweet joy befall thee.

William Blake

A Cradle Song

Sweet dreams, form a shade,
O'er my lovely infant's head!
Sweet dreams of pleasant streams,
By happy, silent, moony beams!

Sweet sleep, with soft down.
Weave thy brows an infant crown!
Sweet sleep, angel mild,
Hover o'er my happy child!

Sweet smiles, in the night
Hover over my delight!
Sweet smiles, mother's smiles,
All the livelong night beguiles.

Sweet moans, dovelike sighs,
Chase not slumber from thy eyes!
Sweet moans, sweeter smiles,
All the dovelike moans beguiles.

Sleep, sleep, happy child!
All creation slept and smiled.
Sleep, sleep, happy sleep.
While o'er thee thy mother weep.

Sweet babe, in thy face,
Holy image I can trace;
Sweet babe, once like thee.
Thy Maker lay, and wept for me:

Wept for me, for thee, for all,
When He was an infant small.
Thou His image ever see,
Heavenly face that smiles on thee!

Smiles on thee, on me, on all,
Who became an infant small;
Infant smiles are His own smiles;
Heaven and earth to peace beguiles.

William Blake

On My First Son

Farewell, thou child of my right hand, and joy;
My sin was too much hope of thee, lov'd boy.
Seven years thou wert lent to me, and I thee pay,
Exacted by thy fate, on the just day.
O, could I lose all father now! For why
Will man lament the state he should envy?
To have so soon 'scap'd world's and flesh's rage,
And if no other misery, yet age?
Rest in soft peace, and, ask'd, say, 'Here doth lie
Ben Jonson his best piece of poetry.'
For whose sake henceforth all his vows be such,
As what he loves may never like too much.

Ben Jonson

My Early Home

Here sparrows build upon the trees,
And stock-dove hides her nest:
The leaves are winnowed by the breeze
Into a calmer rest;
The black-cap's song was very sweet;
That used the rose to kiss;
It made the paradise complete:
My early home was this.

The redbreast from the sweetbrier bush
Dropt down to pick the worm;
On the horse-chestnut sang the thrush,
O'er the house where I was born.
The moonlight, like a shower of pearls,
Fell o'er this 'bower of bliss',
And on the bench sat boys and girls;
My early home was this.

The old house stooped just like a cave,
Thatched o'er with mosses green;
Winter around the walls would rave,
But all was calm within;
The trees are here all green again,
Here bees the flowers still kiss,
But flowers and trees seemed sweeter then;
My early home was this.

John Clare

The First Snow-fall

The snow had begun in the gloaming,
  And busily all the night
Had been heaping field and highway
  With a silence deep and white.

Every pine and fir and hemlock
  Wore ermine too dear for an earl,
And the poorest twig on the elm-tree
  Was ridged inch deep with pearl.

From sheds new-roofed with Carrara
  Came Chanticleer's muffled crow,
The stiff rails were softened to swan's-down,
  And still fluttered down the snow.

I stood and watched by the window
  The noiseless work of the sky,
And the sudden flurries of snow-birds,
  Like brown leaves whirling by.

I thought of a mound in sweet Auburn
  Where a little headstone stood;
How the flakes were folding it gently,
  As did robins the babes in the wood.

Up spoke our own little Mabel,
  Saying, 'Father, who makes it snow?'
And I told of the good All-father
  Who cares for us here below.

Again I looked at the snow-fall,
  And thought of the leaden sky
That arched o'er our first great sorrow,
  When that mound was heaped so high.

I remembered the gradual patience
    That fell from that cloud-like snow,
Flake by flake, healing and hiding
    The scar of our deep-plunged woe.

And again to the child I whispered,
    'The snow that husheth all,
Darling, the merciful Father
    Alone can make it fall!'

Then, with eyes that saw not, I kissed her;
    And she, kissing back, could not know
That *my* kiss was given to her sister,
    Folded close under deepening snow.

James Russell Lowell

The Toys

My little Son, who look'd from thoughtful eyes
And moved and spoke in quiet grown-up wise,
Having my law the seventh time disobey'd,
I struck him, and dismiss'd
With hard words and unkiss'd,
His Mother, who was patient, being dead.
Then, fearing lest his grief should hinder sleep,
I visited his bed,
But found him slumbering deep,
With darken'd eyelids, and their lashes yet
From his late sobbing wet.
And I, with moan,
Kissing away his tears, left others of my own;
For, on a table drawn beside his head,
He had put, within his reach,
A box of counters and a red-vein'd stone,
A piece of glass abraded by the beach
And six or seven shells,
A bottle with bluebells
And two French copper coins, ranged there with careful art,
To comfort his sad heart.
So when that night I pray'd
To God, I wept, and said:
Ah, when at last we lie with tranced breath,
Not vexing Thee in death,
And Thou rememberest of what toys
We made our joys,
How weakly understood
Thy great commanded good,
Then, fatherly not less

Than I whom Thou hast moulded from the clay,
Thou'lt leave Thy wrath, and say,
'I will be sorry for their childishness.'

Coventry Patmore

Home

How brightly glistening in the sun
The woodland ivy plays!
While yonder beeches from their barks
Reflect his silver rays.

That sun surveys a lovely scene
From softly smiling skies;
And wildly through unnumbered trees
The wind of winter sighs:

Now loud, it thunders o'er my head,
And now in distance dies.
But give me back my barren hills
Where colder breezes rise;

Where scarce the scattered, stunted trees
Can yield an answering swell,
But where a wilderness of heath
Returns the sound as well.

For yonder garden, fair and wide,
With groves of evergreen,
Long winding walks, and borders trim,
And velvet lawns between;

Restore to me that little spot,
With grey walls compassed round,
Where knotted grass neglected lies,
And weeds usurp the ground.

Though all around this mansion high
Invites the foot to roam,
And though its halls are fair within–
Oh, give me back my HOME!

Anne Brontë

Sonnet 1 from *Brother and Sister*

I cannot choose but think upon the time
When our two lives grew like two buds that kiss
At lightest thrill from the bee's swinging chime,
Because the one so near the other is.

He was the elder and a little man
Of forty inches, bound to show no dread,
And I the girl that puppy-like now ran,
Now lagged behind my brother's larger tread.

I held him wise, and when he talked to me
Of snakes and birds, and which God loved the best,
I thought his knowledge marked the boundary
Where men grew blind, though angels knew the rest.

If he said Hush! I tried to hold my breath;
Wherever he said Come! I stepped in faith.

George Eliot

Sweet and Low

Sweet and low, sweet and low,
    Wind of the western sea,
Low, low, breathe and blow,
    Wind of the western sea!
Over the rolling waters go,
Come from the dying moon, and blow,
    Blow him again to me;
While my little one, while my pretty one, sleeps.

Sleep and rest, sleep and rest,
    Father will come to thee soon;
Rest, rest, on mother's breast,
    Father will come to thee soon;
Father will come to his babe in the nest,
Silver sails all out of the west
    Under the silver moon:
Sleep, my little one, sleep, my pretty one, sleep.

Alfred, Lord Tennyson

To Ianthe

I love thee, Baby! for thine own sweet sake;
Those azure eyes, that faintly dimpled cheek,
Thy tender frame, so eloquently weak,
Love in the sternest heart of hate might wake;
But more when o'er thy fitful slumber bending
Thy mother folds thee to her wakeful heart,
Whilst love and pity, in her glances blending,
All that thy passive eyes can feel impart:
More, when some feeble lineaments of her,
Who bore thy weight beneath her spotless bosom,
As with deep love I read thy face, recur, –
More dear art thou, O fair and fragile blossom;
Dearest when most thy tender traits express
The image of thy mother's loveliness.

Percy Bysshe Shelley

To My Father on His Birthday

Amidst the days of pleasant mirth,
That throw their halo round our earth;
Amidst the tender thoughts that rise
To call bright tears to happy eyes;
Amidst the silken words that move
To syllable the names we love;
There glides no day of gentle bliss
More soothing to the heart than *this*!
No thoughts of fondness e'er appear
More fond, than those I write of here!
No name can e'er on tablet shine,
My father! more beloved than *thine*!
'Tis sweet, adown the shady past,
A lingering look of love to cast—
Back th' enchanted world to call,
That beamed around us first of all;
And walk with Memory fondly o'er
The paths where Hope had been before—
Sweet to receive the sylphic sound
That breathes in tenderness around,
Repeating to the listening ear
The names that made our childhood dear—
For parted Joy, like Echo, kind,
Will leave her dulcet voice behind,
To tell, amidst the magic air,
How oft she smiled and lingered there.

Elizabeth Barrett Browning

Little Brown Baby

Little brown baby wif spa'klin' eyes,
    Come to yo' pappy an' set on his knee.
What you been doin', suh — makin' san' pies?
    Look at dat bib — you's es du'ty ez me.
Look at dat mouf — dat's merlasses, I bet;
    Come hyeah, Maria, an' wipe off his han's.
Bees gwine to ketch you an' eat you up yit,
    Bein' so sticky an sweet — goodness lan's!

Little brown baby wif spa'klin' eyes,
    Who's pappy's darlin' an' who's pappy's chile?
Who is it all de day nevah once tries
    Fu' to be cross, er once loses dat smile?
Whah did you git dem teef? My, you's a scamp!
    Whah did dat dimple come f'om in yo' chin?
Pappy do' know you — I b'lieves you's a tramp;
    Mammy, dis hyeah's some ol' straggler got in!

Let's th'ow him outen de do' in de san',
    We do' want stragglers a-layin' 'roun' hyeah;
Let's gin him 'way to de big buggah-man;
    I know he's hidin' erroun' hyeah right neah.
Buggah-man, buggah-man, come in de do',
    Hyeah's a bad boy you kin have fu' to eat.
Mammy an' pappy do' want him no mo',
    Swaller him down f'om his haid to his feet!

Dah, now, I t'ought dat you'd hug me up close.
　　Go back, ol' buggah, you sha'n't have dis boy.
He ain't no tramp, ner no straggler, of co'se;
　　He's pappy's pa'dner an' play-mate an' joy.
Come to you' pallet now — go to yo' res';
　　Wisht you could allus know ease an' cleah skies;
Wisht you could stay jes' a chile on my breas'—
　　Little brown baby wif spa'klin' eyes!

Paul Laurence Dunbar

'On the beach at night'

On the beach at night,
Stands a child with her father,
Watching the east, the autumn sky.

Up through the darkness,
While ravening clouds, the burial clouds, in black masses
　　spreading,
Lower sullen and fast athwart and down the sky,
Amid a transparent clear belt of ether yet left in the east,
Ascends large and calm the lord-star Jupiter,
And nigh at hand, only a very little above,
Swim the delicate sisters the Pleiades.

From the beach the child holding the hand of her father,
Those burial-clouds that lower victorious soon to devour all,
Watching, silently weeps.

Weep not, child,
Weep not, my darling,
With these kisses let me remove your tears,
The ravening clouds shall not long be victorious,

They shall not long possess the sky, they devour the stars
 only in apparition,
Jupiter shall emerge, be patient, watch again another night,
 the Pleiades shall emerge,
They are immortal, all those stars both silvery and golden
 shall shine out again,
The great stars and the little ones shall shine out again, they
 endure,
The vast immortal suns and the long-enduring pensive
 moons shall again shine.

Then dearest child mournest thou only for Jupiter?
Considerest thou alone the burial of the stars?

Something there is,
(With my lips soothing thee, adding I whisper,
I give thee the first suggestion, the problem and indirection,)
Something there is more immortal even than the stars,
(Many the burials, many the days and nights, passing away,)
Something that shall endure longer even than lustrous
 Jupiter
Longer than sun or any revolving satellite,
Or the radiant sisters the Pleiades.

Walt Whitman

Mother and Babe

I see the sleeping babe, nestling the breast of its
 mother;
The sleeping mother and babe—hush'd, I study them
 long and long.

Walt Whitman

29

Rock Me To Sleep

Backward, turn backward, O Time, in your flight,
Make me a child again just for tonight!
Mother, come back from the echoless shore,
Take me again to your heart as of yore;
Kiss from my forehead the furrows of care,
Smooth the few silver threads out of my hair;
Over my slumbers your loving watch keep;—
Rock me to sleep, mother, – rock me to sleep!

Backward, flow backward, O tide of the years!
I am so weary of toil and of tears,—
Toil without recompense, tears all in vain,—
Take them, and give me my childhood again!
I have grown weary of dust and decay,—
Weary of flinging my soul-wealth away;
Weary of sowing for others to reap;—
Rock me to sleep, mother – rock me to sleep!

Tired of the hollow, the base, the untrue,
Mother, O mother, my heart calls for you!
Many a summer the grass has grown green,
Blossomed and faded, our faces between:
Yet, with strong yearning and passionate pain,
Long I tonight for your presence again.
Come from the silence so long and so deep;—
Rock me to sleep, mother, – rock me to sleep!

Over my heart, in the days that are flown,
No love like mother-love ever has shone;
No other worship abides and endures,—
Faithful, unselfish, and patient like yours:
None like a mother can charm away pain
From the sick soul and the world-weary brain.
Slumber's soft calms o'er my heavy lids creep;—
Rock me to sleep, mother, – rock me to sleep!

Come, let your brown hair, just lighted with gold,
Fall on your shoulders again as of old;
Let it drop over my forehead tonight,
Shading my faint eyes away from the light;
For with its sunny-edged shadows once more
Haply will throng the sweet visions of yore;
Lovingly, softly, its bright billows sweep;—
Rock me to sleep, mother, – rock me to sleep!

Mother, dear mother, the years have been long
Since I last listened your lullaby song:
Sing, then, and unto my soul it shall seem
Womanhood's years have been only a dream.
Clasped to your heart in a loving embrace,
With your light lashes just sweeping my face,
Never hereafter to wake or to weep;—
Rock me to sleep, mother, – rock me to sleep!

Elizabeth Akers Allen

'One Sister have I in our house'

One Sister have I in our house –
And one a hedge away.
There's only one recorded,
But both belong to me.

One came the way that I came –
And wore my past year's gown –
The other as a bird her nest,
Builded our hearts among.

She did not sing as we did –
It was a different tune –
Herself to her a Music
As Bumble-bee of June.

Today is far from Childhood –
But up and down the hills
I held her hand the tighter –
Which shortened all the miles –

And still her hum
The years among,
Deceives the Butterfly;
Still in her Eye
The Violets lie
Mouldered this many May.

I spilt the dew –
But took the morn, –
I chose this single star
From out the wide night's numbers –
Sue – forevermore!

Emily Dickinson

32

A Question

Why is it, God, that mothers' hearts are made
So very deep and wide?
How does it help the world that we should hold
Such swelling floods of pain till we are old,
Because when we were young one grave was laid –
One baby died?

Charlotte Perkins Gilman

My Grandmother's Love Letters

There are no stars tonight
But those of memory.
Yet how much room for memory there is
In the loose girdle of soft rain.

There is even room enough
For the letters of my mother's mother,
Elizabeth,
That have been pressed so long
Into a corner of the roof
That they are brown and soft,
And liable to melt as snow.

Over the greatness of such space
Steps must be gentle.
It is all hung by an invisible white hair.
It trembles as birch limbs webbing the air.

And I ask myself:

'Are your fingers long enough to play
Old keys that are but echoes:
Is the silence strong enough
To carry back the music to its source
And back to you again
As though to her?'

Yet I would lead my grandmother by the hand
Through much of what she would not understand;
And so I stumble. And the rain continues on the roof
With such a sound of gently pitying laughter.

Hart Crane

The Birthnight: to F

Dearest, it was a night
That in its darkness rocked Orion's stars;
A sighing wind ran faintly white
Along the willows, and the cedar boughs
Laid their wide hands in stealthy peace across
The starry silence of their antique moss:
No sound save rushing air
Cold, yet all sweet with Spring,
And in thy mother's arms, couched weeping there,
Thou, lovely thing.

Walter de la Mare

Growing Up
and Growing Older

Baby

Where did you come from, baby dear?
Out of the everywhere into here.

Where did you get your eyes so blue?
Out of the sky as I came through.

What makes the light in them sparkle and spin?
Some of the starry spikes left in.

Where did you get that little tear?
I found it waiting when I got here.

What makes your forehead so smooth and high?
A soft hand stroked it as I went by.

What makes your cheek like a warm white rose?
I saw something better than anyone knows.

Whence that three-cornered smile of bliss?
Three angels gave me at once a kiss.

Where did you get this pearly ear?
God spoke, and it came out to hear.

Where did you get those arms and hands?
Love made itself into hooks and bands.

Feet, whence did you come, you darling things?
From the same box as the cherubs' wings.

How did they all just come to be you?
God thought about me, and so I grew.

But how did you come to us, you dear?
God thought about you, and so I am here.

George Macdonald

Answer to a Child's Question

Do you ask what the birds say? The Sparrow, the Dove,
The Linnet and Thrush say, 'I love and I love!'
In the winter they're silent—the wind is so strong;
What it says, I don't know, but it sings a loud song.
But green leaves, and blossoms, and sunny warm weather,
And singing, and loving—all come back together.
But the Lark is so brimful of gladness and love,
The green fields below him, the blue sky above,
That he sings, and he sings; and for ever sings he—
'I love my Love, and my Love loves me!'

Samuel Taylor Coleridge

The First Tooth

Through the house what busy joy,
Just because the infant boy
Has a tiny tooth to show!
I have got a double row,
All as white, and all as small;
Yet no one cares for mine at all.
He can say but half a word,
Yet that single sound's preferred
To all the words that I can say
In the longest summer day.
He cannot walk, yet if he put
With mimic motion out his foot,
As if he thought he were advancing,
It's prized more than my best dancing.

Charles and Mary Lamb

My Shadow

I have a little shadow that goes in and out with me,
And what can be the use of him is more than I can see.
He is very, very like me from the heels up to the head;
And I see him jump before me, when I jump into my bed.

The funniest thing about him is the way he likes to grow—
Not at all like proper children, which is always very slow;
For he sometimes shoots up taller like an india-rubber ball,
And he sometimes gets so little that there's none of him at all.

He hasn't got a notion of how children ought to play,
And can only make a fool of me in every sort of way.
He stays so close beside me, he's a coward you can see;
I'd think shame to stick to nursie as that shadow sticks to me!

One morning, very early, before the sun was up,
I rose and found the shining dew on every buttercup;
But my lazy little shadow, like an arrant sleepy-head,
Had stayed at home behind me and was fast asleep in bed.

Robert Louis Stevenson

Spring and Fall: to a young child

Márgarét, áre you gríeving
Over Goldengrove unleaving?
Leáves like the things of man, you
With your fresh thoughts care for, can you?
Ah! ás the heart grows older
It will come to such sights colder
By and by, nor spare a sigh
Though worlds of wanwood leafmeal lie;
And yet you wíll weep and know why.
Now no matter, child, the name:
Sórrow's spríngs áre the same.
Nor mouth had, no nor mind, expressed
What heart heard of, ghost guessed:
It ís the blight man was born for,
It is Margaret you mourn for.

Gerard Manley Hopkins

The Lost Doll

I once had a sweet little doll, dears,
The prettiest doll in the world;
Her cheeks were so red and so white, dears,
And her hair was so charmingly curled.
But I lost my poor little doll, dears,
As I played in the heath one day;
And I cried for more than a week, dears,
But I never could find where she lay.

I found my poor little doll, dears,
As I played in the heath one day:
Folks say she is terribly changed, dears,
For her paint is all washed away,
And her arms trodden off by the cows, dears
And her hair not the least bit curled:
Yet for old sakes' sake she is still, dears,
The prettiest doll in the world.

Charles Kingsley

She Being Young

The home of love is her blue eyes,
Wherein all joy, all beauty lies,
More sweet than hopes of paradise,
    She being young.

Speak of her with a miser's praise;
She craves no golden speech; her ways
Wind through charmed nights and magic days,
    She being young.

She is so far from pain and death,
So warm her cheek, so sweet her breath
Glad words are all the words she saith,
    She being young.

Seeing her face, it seems not far
To Troy's heroic field of war,
To Troy and all great things that are,
    She being young.

John Charles McNeill

Youth and June

I was your lover long ago, sweet June,
Ere life grew hard; I am your lover still,
And follow gladly to the wondrous tune
You pipe on golden reeds to vale and hill.
I am your lover still; to me you seem

To hold the fragrance of the joys long dead,
The brightness and the beauty of the dream
We dreamed in youth, to hold the tears we shed,
The laughter of our lips, the faith that lies
Back in that season dear to every heart,
Life's springtime, when God's earth and God's blue skies
Are, measured by our glance, not far apart.

Jean Blewett

'When I was one-and-twenty'

When I was one-and-twenty
    I heard a wise man say,
'Give crowns and pounds and guineas
    But not your heart away;
Give pearls away and rubies
    But keep your fancy free.'
But I was one-and-twenty,
    No use to talk to me.

When I was one-and-twenty
    I heard him say again,
'The heart out of the bosom
    Was never given in vain;
'Tis paid with sighs a plenty
    And sold for endless rue.'
And I am two-and-twenty,
    And oh, 'tis true, 'tis true.

A. E. Housman

A Madrigal

Crabbed Age and Youth
Cannot live together:
Youth is full of pleasance,
Age is full of care;
Youth like summer morn,
Age like winter weather,
Youth like summer brave,
Age like winter bare:
Youth is full of sport,
Age's breath is short,
Youth is nimble, Age is lame:
Youth is hot and bold,
Age is weak and cold,
Youth is wild, and Age is tame:—
Age, I do abhor thee,
Youth, I do adore thee;
O! my Love, my Love is young!
Age, I do defy thee—
O sweet shepherd, hie thee,
For methinks thou stay'st too long.

William Shakespeare

'I remember, I remember'

I remember, I remember,
The house where I was born,
The little window where the sun
Came peeping in at morn;

He never came a wink too soon,
Nor brought too long a day,
But now, I often wish the night
Had borne my breath away!

I remember, I remember,
The roses, red and white,
The vi'lets, and the lily-cups,
Those flowers made of light!
The lilacs where the robin built,
And where my brother set
The laburnum on his birthday,—
The tree is living yet!

I remember, I remember,
Where I was used to swing,
And thought the air must rush as fresh
To swallows on the wing;
My spirit flew in feathers then,
That is so heavy now,
And summer pools could hardly cool
The fever on my brow!

I remember, I remember,
The fir trees dark and high;
I used to think their slender tops
Were close against the sky:
It was a childish ignorance,
But now 'tis little joy
To know I'm farther off from heav'n
Than when I was a boy.

Thomas Hood

Piano

Softly, in the dusk, a woman is singing to me;
Taking me back down the vista of years, till I see
A child sitting under the piano, in the boom of the tingling
    strings
And pressing the small, poised feet of a mother who smiles
    as she sings.
In spite of myself, the insidious mastery of song
Betrays me back, till the heart of me weeps to belong
To the old Sunday evenings at home, with winter outside
And hymns in the cosy parlour, the tinkling piano our guide.

So now it is vain for the singer to burst into clamour
With the great black piano appassionato. The glamour
Of childish days is upon me, my manhood is cast
Down in the flood of remembrance, I weep like a child
for the past.

D. H. Lawrence

You Are Old, Father William

'You are old, Father William,' the young man said,
'And your hair has become very white;
And yet you incessantly stand on your head –
Do you think, at your age, it is right?'

'In my youth,' Father William replied to his son,
'I feared it might injure the brain;
But, now that I'm perfectly sure I have none,
Why, I do it again and again.'

'You are old,' said the youth, 'as I mentioned before,
And have grown most uncommonly fat;
Yet you turned a back-somersault in at the door –
Pray, what is the reason of that?'

'In my youth,' said the sage, as he shook his grey locks,
'I kept all my limbs very supple
By the use of this ointment – one shilling the box –
Allow me to sell you a couple?'

'You are old,' said the youth, 'and your jaws are too weak
For anything tougher than suet;
Yet you finished the goose, with the bones and the beak –
Pray how did you manage to do it?'

'In my youth,' said his father, 'I took to the law,
And argued each case with my wife;
And the muscular strength, which it gave to my jaw,
Has lasted the rest of my life.'

'You are old,' said the youth, 'one would hardly suppose
That your eye was as steady as ever;
Yet you balanced an eel on the end of your nose –
What made you so awfully clever?'

'I have answered three questions, and that is enough,'
Said his father; 'don't give yourself airs!
Do you think I can listen all day to such stuff?
Be off, or I'll kick you downstairs!'

Lewis Carroll

Jenny Kissed Me

Jenny kiss'd me when we met,
    Jumping from the chair she sat in;
Time, you thief, who love to get
    Sweets into your list, put that in!
Say I'm weary, say I'm sad,
    Say that health and wealth have miss'd me,
Say I'm growing old, but add,
    Jenny kiss'd me.

Leigh Hunt

'Loveliest of trees, the cherry now'

Loveliest of trees, the cherry now
Is hung with bloom along the bough,
And stands about the woodland ride
Wearing white for Eastertide.

Now, of my threescore years and ten,
Twenty will not come again,
And take from seventy springs a score,
It only leaves me fifty more.

And since to look at things in bloom
Fifty springs are little room,
About the woodlands I will go
To see the cherry hung with snow.

A. E. Housman

On One Who Lived and Died Where He Was Born

When a night in November
Blew forth its bleared airs
An infant descended
His birth-chamber stairs
For the very first time,
At the still, midnight chime;
All unapprehended
His mission, his aim.–
Thus, first, one November,
An infant descended
The stairs.

On a night in November
Of weariful cares,
A frail aged figure
Ascended those stairs
For the very last time:
All gone his life's prime,
All vanished his vigour,
And fine, forceful frame:
Thus, last, one November
Ascended that figure
Upstairs.

On those nights in November –
Apart eighty years –
The babe and the bent one
Who traversed those stairs
From the early first time
To the last feeble climb –
That fresh and that spent one –
Were even the same:
Yea, who passed in November
As infant, as bent one,
Those stairs.

Wise child of November!
From birth to blanched hairs
Descending, ascending,
Wealth-wantless, those stairs;
Who saw quick in time
As a vain pantomime
Life's tending, its ending,
The worth of its fame.
Wise child of November,
Descending, ascending
Those stairs!

Thomas Hardy

When You Are Old

When you are old and grey and full of sleep,
And nodding by the fire, take down this book,
And slowly read, and dream of the soft look
Your eyes had once, and of their shadows deep;

How many loved your moments of glad grace,
And loved your beauty with love false or true,
But one man loved the pilgrim soul in you,
And loved the sorrows of your changing face;

And bending down beside the glowing bars,
Murmur, a little sadly, how Love fled
And paced upon the mountains overhead
And hid his face amid a crowd of stars.

W. B. Yeats

The Pleiades

By day you cannot see the sky
For it is up so very high.
You look and look, but it's so blue
That you can never see right through.

But when night comes it is quite plain,
And all the stars are there again.
They seem just like old friends to me,
I've known them all my life you see.

There is the dipper first, and there
Is Cassiopeia in her chair,
Orion's belt, the Milky Way,
And lots I know but cannot say.

One group looks like a swarm of bees,
Papa says they're the Pleiades;
But I think they must be the toy
Of some nice little angel boy.

Perhaps his jackstones which to-day
He has forgot to put away,
And left them lying on the sky
Where he will find them bye and bye.

I wish he'd come and play with me.
We'd have such fun, for it would be
A most unusual thing for boys
To feel that they had stars for toys.

Amy Lowell

Childhood

I used to think that grown-up people chose
To have stiff backs and wrinkles round their nose,
And veins like small fat snakes on either hand,
On purpose to be grand.
Till through the banister I watched one day
My great-aunt Etty's friend who was going away,
And how her onyx beads had come unstrung.
I saw her grope to find them as they rolled;
And then I knew that she was helplessly old,
As I was helplessly young.

Frances Darwin Cornford

Love

'There is a lady sweet and kind'

There is a lady sweet and kind,
Was never face so pleas'd my mind;
I did but see her passing by,
And yet I love her till I die.

Her gesture, motion, and her smiles,
Her wit, her voice, my heart beguiles,
Beguiles my heart, I know not why,
And yet I love her till I die.

Her free behaviour, winning looks,
Will make a lawyer burn his books;
I touch'd her not, alas! not I,
And yet I love her till I die.

Had I her fast betwixt mine arms,
Judge you that think such sports were harms,
Were't any harm? no, no, fie, fie,
For I will love her till I die.

Should I remain confined there
So long as Phoebus in his sphere,
I to request, she to deny,
Yet would I love her till I die.

Cupid is winged and doth range,
Her country so my love doth change:
But change she earth, or change she sky,
Yet will I love her till I die.

Attributed to Thomas Ford

'One day I wrote her name upon the strand'

One day I wrote her name upon the strand,
But came the waves and washèd it away:
Again I wrote it with a second hand,
But came the tide and made my pains his prey.
Vain man (said she) that dost in vain assay
A mortal thing so to immortalise;
For I myself shall like to this decay,
And eke my name be wipèd out likewise.
Not so (quod I); let baser things devise
To die in dust, but you shall live by fame;
My verse your virtues rare shall eternise,
And in the heavens write your glorious name:
Where, when as Death shall all the world subdue,
Our love shall live, and later life renew.

Edmund Spenser

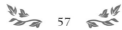

The Sun Rising

Busy old fool, unruly Sun,
      Why dost thou thus,
Through windows, and through curtains, call on us?
Must to thy motions lovers' seasons run?
      Saucy pedantic wretch, go chide
      Late school-boys and sour prentices,
    Go tell court-huntsmen that the king will ride,
    Call country ants to harvest offices;
Love, all alike, no season knows nor clime,
Nor hours, days, months, which are the rags of time.

      Thy beams so reverend, and strong
      Why shouldst thou think?
I could eclipse and cloud them with a wink,
But that I would not lose her sight so long.
      If her eyes have not blinded thine,
      Look, and to-morrow late tell me,
    Whether both th' Indias of spice and mine
    Be where thou left'st them, or lie here with me.
Ask for those kings whom thou saw'st yesterday,
And thou shalt hear, "All here in one bed lay."

      She's all states, and all princes I;
      Nothing else is;
Princes do but play us; compared to this,
All honour's mimic, all wealth alchemy.
      Thou, Sun, art half as happy as we,
      In that the world's contracted thus;
    Thine age asks ease, and since thy duties be
    To warm the world, that's done in warming us.
Shine here to us, and thou art everywhere;
This bed thy centre is, these walls thy sphere.

John Donne

58

'Can Life be a Blessing?'
from *Troilus and Cressida*

Can Life be a Blessing,
    Or worth the possessing,
Can Life be a blessing if Love were away?
  Ah no! though our Love all Night keep us waking,
And though he torment us with Cares all the Day,
  Yet he sweetens he sweetens our Pains in the taking,
There's an Hour at the last, there's an Hour to repay.

    In ev'ry possessing,
    The ravishing Blessing,
In ev'ry possessing the Fruit of our Pain,
  Poor Lovers forget long Ages of Anguish,
What e're they have suffer'd and done to obtain;
  'Tis a Pleasure, a Pleasure to sigh and to languish,
When we hope, when we hope to be happy again.

John Dryden

From *The Rubaiyat* of Omar Khayyam

A book of Verses underneath the Bough,
A Jug of Wine, a Loaf of Bread—and Thou
    Beside me singing in the Wilderness—
O, Wilderness were Paradise enow!

Trans. Edward Fitzgerald

A Thousand Martyrs

A thousand martyrs I have made,
    All sacrificed to my desire;
A thousand beauties have betrayed,
    That languish in resistless fire.
The untamed heart to hand I brought,
And fixed the wild and wandering thought.

I never vowed nor sighed in vain
    But both, though false, were well received.
The fair are pleased to give us pain,
    And what they wish is soon believed.
And though I talked of wounds and smart,
Love's pleasures only touched my heart.

Alone the glory and the spoil
    I always laughing bore away;
The triumphs, without pain or toil,
    Without the hell, the heav'n of joy.
And while I thus at random rove
Despise the fools that whine for love.

Aphra Behn

Sonnet 'Let me not to the marriage of true minds'

Let me not to the marriage of true minds
Admit impediments. Love is not love
Which alters when it alteration finds,
Or bends with the remover to remove:
O no; it is an ever-fixed mark,

That looks on tempests, and is never shaken;
It is the star to every wandering bark,
Whose worth's unknown, although his height be taken.
Love's not Time's fool, though rosy lips and cheeks
Within his bending sickle's compass come;
Love alters not with his brief hours and weeks,
But bears it out even to the edge of doom.
    If this be error and upon me proved,
    I never writ, nor no man ever loved.

William Shakespeare

The Passionate Shepherd to His Love

Come live with me and be my Love,
And we will all the pleasures prove
That hills and valleys, dale and field,
And all the craggy mountains yield.

There will we sit upon the rocks
And see the shepherds feed their flocks,
By shallow rivers, to whose falls
Melodious birds sing madrigals.

There will I make thee beds of roses
And a thousand fragrant posies,
A cap of flowers, and a kirtle
Embroider'd all with leaves of myrtle.

A gown made of the finest wool
Which from our pretty lambs we pull,
Fair linèd slippers for the cold,
With buckles of the purest gold.

A belt of straw and ivy buds
With coral clasps and amber studs:
And if these pleasures may thee move,
Come live with me and be my Love.

Thy silver dishes for thy meat
As precious as the gods do eat,
Shall on an ivory table be
Prepared each day for thee and me.

The shepherd swains shall dance and sing
For thy delight each May-morning:
If these delights thy mind may move,
Then live with me and be my Love.

Christopher Marlowe

The Nymph's Reply to the Shepherd

If all the world and love were young,
And truth in every Shepherd's tongue,
These pretty pleasures might me move,
To live with thee, and be thy love.

Time drives the flocks from field to fold,
When Rivers rage and Rocks grow cold,
And Philomel becometh dumb,
The rest complains of cares to come.

The flowers do fade, and wanton fields,
To wayward winter reckoning yields,
A honey tongue, a heart of gall,
Is fancy's spring, but sorrow's fall.

Thy gowns, thy shoes, thy beds of Roses,
Thy cap, thy kirtle, and thy posies
Soon break, soon wither, soon forgotten:
In folly ripe, in reason rotten.

Thy belt of straw and Ivy buds,
The Coral clasps and amber studs,
All these in me no means can move
To come to thee and be thy love.

But could youth last, and love still breed,
Had joys no date, nor age no need,
Then these delights my mind might move
To live with thee, and be thy love.

Sir Walter Raleigh

To His Coy Mistress

Had we but world enough and time,
This coyness, lady, were no crime.
We would sit down, and think which way
To walk, and pass our long love's day.
Thou by the Indian Ganges' side
Shouldst rubies find; I by the tide
Of Humber would complain. I would
Love you ten years before the flood,
And you should, if you please, refuse
Till the conversion of the Jews.
My vegetable love should grow
Vaster than empires and more slow;
An hundred years should go to praise
Thine eyes, and on thy forehead gaze;
Two hundred to adore each breast,
But thirty thousand to the rest;
An age at least to every part,
And the last age should show your heart.
For, lady, you deserve this state,
Nor would I love at lower rate.

But at my back I always hear
Time's wingèd chariot hurrying near;
And yonder all before us lie
Deserts of vast eternity.

Thy beauty shall no more be found;
Nor, in thy marble vault, shall sound
My echoing song; then worms shall try
That long-preserved virginity,
And your quaint honour turn to dust,
And into ashes all my lust;
The grave's a fine and private place,
But none, I think, do there embrace.
    Now therefore, while the youthful hue
Sits on thy skin like morning dew,
And while thy willing soul transpires
At every pore with instant fires,
Now let us sport us while we may,
And now, like amorous birds of prey,
Rather at once our time devour
Than languish in his slow-chapped power.
Let us roll all our strength and all
Our sweetness up into one ball,
And tear our pleasures with rough strife
Through the iron gates of life:
Thus, though we cannot make our sun
Stand still, yet we will make him run.

Andrew Marvell

A Red, Red Rose

O my Luve's like a red, red rose,
That's newly sprung in June:
O my Luve's like the melodie,
That's sweetly play'd in tune.

As fair art thou, my bonnie lass,
So deep in luve am I;
And I will luve thee still, my dear,
Till a' the seas gang dry.

Till a' the seas gang dry, my dear,
And the rocks melt wi' the sun;
And I will luve thee still, my dear,
While the sands o' life shall run.

And fare-thee-weel, my only Luve!
And fare-thee-weel, a while!
And I will come again, my Luve,
Tho' 'twere ten thousand mile!

Robert Burns

Love's Philosophy

The fountains mingle with the river
    And the rivers with the ocean,
The winds of heaven mix for ever
    With a sweet emotion;
Nothing in the world is single;
    All things by a law divine
In one spirit meet and mingle.
    Why not I with thine?—

See the mountains kiss high heaven
    And the waves clasp one another;
No sister-flower would be forgiven
    If it disdained its brother;
And the sunlight clasps the earth
    And the moonbeams kiss the sea:
What is all this sweet work worth
    If thou kiss not me?

Percy Bysshe Shelley

How Do I Love Thee?

How do I love thee? Let me count the ways.
I love thee to the depth and breadth and height
My soul can reach, when feeling out of sight
For the ends of being and ideal grace.
I love thee to the level of every day's
Most quiet need, by sun and candle-light.
I love thee freely, as men strive for right.
I love thee purely, as they turn from praise.
I love thee with the passion put to use
In my old griefs, and with my childhood's faith.
I love thee with a love I seemed to lose
With my lost saints. I love thee with the breath,
Smiles, tears, of all my life; and, if God choose,
I shall but love thee better after death.

Elizabeth Barrett Browning

67

She Walks in Beauty

She walks in beauty, like the night
    Of cloudless climes and starry skies;
And all that's best of dark and bright
    Meet in her aspect and her eyes;
Thus mellowed to that tender light
    Which heaven to gaudy day denies.

One shade the more, one ray the less,
    Had half impaired the nameless grace
Which waves in every raven tress,
    Or softly lightens o'er her face;
Where thoughts serenely sweet express,
    How pure, how dear their dwelling-place.

And on that cheek, and o'er that brow,
    So soft, so calm, yet eloquent,
The smiles that win, the tints that glow,
    But tell of days in goodness spent,
A mind at peace with all below,
    A heart whose love is innocent!

Lord Byron

We'll Go No More A Roving

So, we'll go no more a roving
    So late into the night,
Though the heart be still as loving,
    And the moon be still as bright.

For the sword outwears its sheath,
    And the soul wears out the breast,
And the heart must pause to breathe,
    And love itself have rest.

Though the night was made for loving,
    And the day returns too soon,
Yet we'll go no more a roving
    By the light of the moon.

Lord Byron

Bright Star

Bright star, would I were stedfast as thou art—
    Not in lone splendour hung aloft the night
And watching, with eternal lids apart,
    Like nature's patient, sleepless Eremite,
The moving waters at their priestlike task
    Of pure ablution round earth's human shores,
Or gazing on the new soft-fallen mask
    Of snow upon the mountains and the moors—
No—yet still stedfast, still unchangeable,
    Pillow'd upon my fair love's ripening breast,
To feel for ever its soft fall and swell,
    Awake for ever in a sweet unrest,
Still, still to hear her tender-taken breath,
And so live ever—or else swoon to death.

John Keats

69

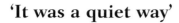

'It was a quiet way'

It was a quiet way –
He asked if I was his –
I made no answer of the Tongue
But answer of the Eyes –
And then He bore me on
Before this mortal noise
With swiftness, as of Chariots
And distance, as of Wheels.
This World did drop away
As Acres from the feet
Of one that leaneth from Balloon
Upon an Ether street.
The Gulf behind was not,
The Continents were new –
Eternity it was before
Eternity was due.
No Seasons were to us –
It was not Night nor Morn –
But Sunrise stopped upon the place
And fastened it in Dawn.

Emily Dickinson

'I am in love, meantime, you think' from *Amours de Voyage*

I am in love, meantime, you think; no doubt you would
 think so.
I am in love, you say; with those letters, of course, you would
 say so.
I am in love, you declare. I think not so; yet I grant you
It is a pleasure indeed to converse with this girl. Oh, rare gift,
Rare felicity, this! she can talk in a rational way, can
Speak upon subjects that really are matters of mind and of
 thinking,
Yet in perfection retain her simplicity; never, one moment,
Never, however you urge it, however you tempt her,
 consents to
Step from ideas and fancies and loving sensations to
 those vain
Conscious understandings that vex the minds of mankind.
No, though she talk, it is music; her fingers desert not the
 keys; 'tis
Song, though you hear in the song the articulate vocables
 sounded,
Syllabled singly and sweetly the words of melodious
 meaning.
I am in love, you say; I do not think so, exactly.

Arthur Hugh Clough

Meeting at Night

The grey sea and the long black land;
And the yellow half-moon large and low;
And the startled little waves that leap
In fiery ringlets from their sleep,
As I gain the cove with pushing prow,
And quench its speed i' the slushy sand.

Then a mile of warm sea-scented beach;
Three fields to cross till a farm appears;
A tap at the pane, the quick sharp scratch
And blue spurt of a lighted match,
And a voice less loud, thro' its joys and fears,
Than the two hearts beating each to each!

Robert Browning

Sudden Light

I have been here before,
        But when or how I cannot tell:
    I know the grass beyond the door,
        The sweet keen smell,
The sighing sound, the lights around the shore.

    You have been mine before,—
        How long ago I may not know:
    But just when at that swallow's soar
        Your neck turn'd so,
Some veil did fall,—I knew it all of yore.

Has this been thus before?
     And shall not thus time's eddying flight
Still with our lives our love restore
     In death's despite,
And day and night yield one delight once more?

Dante Gabriel Rossetti

'I loved you first: but afterwards your love'

Poca favilla gran fiamma seconda. – Dante
Ogni altra cosa, ogni pensier va fore,
E sol ivi con voi rimansi amore. – Petrarca

I loved you first: but afterwards your love
  Outsoaring mine, sang such a loftier song
As drowned the friendly cooings of my dove.
  Which owes the other most? my love was long,
  And yours one moment seemed to wax more strong;
I loved and guessed at you, you construed me
And loved me for what might or might not be –
  Nay, weights and measures do us both a wrong.
For verily love knows not 'mine' or 'thine;'
  With separate 'I' and 'thou' free love has done,
    For one is both and both are one in love:
Rich love knows nought of 'thine that is not mine;'
    Both have the strength and both the length thereof,
Both of us, of the love which makes us one.

Christina Rossetti

The Voice

Woman much missed, how you call to me, call to me,
Saying that now you are not as you were
When you had changed from the one who was all to me,
But as at first, when our day was fair.

Can it be you that I hear? Let me view you, then,
Standing as when I drew near to the town
Where you would wait for me: yes, as I knew you then,
Even to the original air-blue gown!

Or is it only the breeze, in its listlessness
Travelling across the wet mead to me here,
You being ever dissolved to wan wistlessness,
Heard no more again far or near?

    Thus I; faltering forward,
    Leaves around me falling,
Wind oozing thin through the thorn from norward,
    And the woman calling.

Thomas Hardy

Animals and
Nature

The Flea

Mark but this flea, and mark in this,
How little that which thou deniest me is;
It sucked me first, and now sucks thee,
And in this flea our two bloods mingled be;
Thou know'st that this cannot be said
A sin, nor shame, nor loss of maidenhead,
    Yet this enjoys before it woo,
      And pampered swells with one blood made of two,
      And this, alas, is more than we would do.

Oh stay, three lives in one flea spare,
Where we almost, nay more than married are.
This flea is you and I, and this
Our marriage bed, and marriage temple is;
Though parents grudge, and you, w'are met,
And cloistered in these living walls of jet.
    Though use make you apt to kill me,
      Let not to that, self-murder added be,
      And sacrilege, three sins in killing three.

Cruel and sudden, hast thou since
Purpled thy nail, in blood of innocence?
Wherein could this flea guilty be,
Except in that drop which it sucked from thee?
Yet thou triumph'st, and say'st that thou
Find'st not thy self, nor me the weaker now;
    'Tis true; then learn how false, fears be:
      Just so much honor, when thou yield'st to me,
      Will waste, as this flea's death took life from thee.

John Donne

The Tyger

Tyger Tyger, burning bright,
In the forests of the night;
What immortal hand or eye,
Could frame thy fearful symmetry?

In what distant deeps or skies.
Burnt the fire of thine eyes?
On what wings dare he aspire?
What the hand, dare seize the fire?

And what shoulder, & what art,
Could twist the sinews of thy heart?
And when thy heart began to beat,
What dread hand? & what dread feet?

What the hammer? what the chain,
In what furnace was thy brain?
What the anvil? what dread grasp,
Dare its deadly terrors clasp!

When the stars threw down their spears
And water'd heaven with their tears:
Did he smile his work to see?
Did he who made the Lamb make thee?

Tyger Tyger burning bright,
In the forests of the night:
What immortal hand or eye,
Dare frame thy fearful symmetry?

William Blake

Daffodils

I wander'd lonely as a cloud
That floats on high o'er vales and hills,
When all at once I saw a crowd,
A host of golden daffodils,
Beside the lake, beneath the trees
Fluttering and dancing in the breeze.
Continuous as the stars that shine
And twinkle on the milky way,
They stretch'd in never-ending line
Along the margin of a bay:
Ten thousand saw I at a glance
Tossing their heads in sprightly dance.
The waves beside them danced, but they
Out-did the sparkling waves in glee: —
A poet could not but be gay
In such a jocund company!

I gazed – and gazed – but little thought
What wealth the show to me had brought.
For oft, when on my couch I lie
In vacant or in pensive mood,
They flash upon that inward eye
Which is the bliss of solitude;
And then my heart with pleasure fills
And dances with the daffodils.

William Wordsworth

On a Lane in Spring

A Little Lane, the brook runs close beside
And spangles in the sunshine while the fish glide swiftly by
And hedges leafing with the green spring tide
From out their greenery the old birds fly
And chirp and whistle in the morning sun
The pilewort glitters 'neath the pale blue sky
The little robin has its nest begun
And grass green linnets round the bushes fly
How Mild the Spring Comes in; the daisy buds
Lift up their golden blossoms to the sky
How lovely are the pingles and the woods
Here a beetle runs; and there a fly
Rests on the Arum leaf in bottle green
And all the Spring in this Sweet lane is seen.

John Clare

To Autumn

Season of mists and mellow fruitfulness,
    Close bosom-friend of the maturing sun;
Conspiring with him how to load and bless
    With fruit the vines that round the thatch-eves run;
To bend with apples the moss'd cottage-trees,
    And fill all fruit with ripeness to the core;
        To swell the gourd, and plump the hazel shells
With a sweet kernel; to set budding more,
    And still more, later flowers for the bees,
    Until they think warm days will never cease,
        For Summer has o'er-brimm'd their clammy cells.

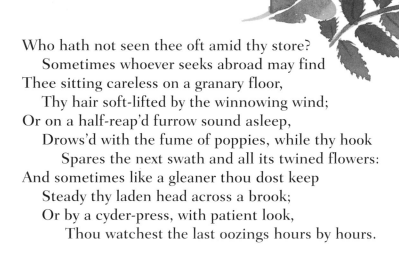

Who hath not seen thee oft amid thy store?
    Sometimes whoever seeks abroad may find
Thee sitting careless on a granary floor,
    Thy hair soft-lifted by the winnowing wind;
Or on a half-reap'd furrow sound asleep,
    Drows'd with the fume of poppies, while thy hook
        Spares the next swath and all its twined flowers:
And sometimes like a gleaner thou dost keep
    Steady thy laden head across a brook;
    Or by a cyder-press, with patient look,
        Thou watchest the last oozings hours by hours.

Where are the songs of Spring? Ay, where are they?
　　Think not of them, thou hast thy music too,—
While barred clouds bloom the soft-dying day,
　　And touch the stubble plains with rosy hue;
Then in a wailful choir the small gnats mourn
　　Among the river sallows, borne aloft
　　　　Or sinking as the light wind lives or dies;
And full-grown lambs loud bleat from hilly bourn;
　　Hedge-crickets sing; and now with treble soft
　　The red-breast whistles from a garden-croft;
　　　　And gathering swallows twitter in the skies.

John Keats

To the Grasshopper and the Cricket

Green little vaulter in the sunny grass,
Catching your heart up at the feel of June,
Sole voice that's heard amidst the lazy noon,
When even the bees lag at the summoning brass;
And you, warm little housekeeper, who class
With those who think the candles come too soon,
Loving the fire, and with your tricksome tune
Nick the glad silent moments as they pass;
Oh sweet and tiny cousins, that belong
One to the fields, the other to the hearth,
Both have your sunshine; both, though small, are strong
At your clear hearts; and both were sent on earth
To sing in thoughtful ears this natural song:
Indoors and out, summer and winter, – Mirth.

Leigh Hunt

81

'A Bird came down the Walk'

A Bird came down the Walk—
He did not know I saw—
He bit an Angleworm in halves
And ate the fellow, raw,

And then he drank a Dew
From a convenient Grass—
And then hopped sidewise to the Wall
To let a Beetle pass—

He glanced with rapid eyes
That hurried all around—
They looked like frightened Beads, I thought—
He stirred his Velvet Head

Like one in danger, Cautious,
I offered him a Crumb
And he unrolled his feathers
And rowed him softer home—

Than Oars divide the Ocean,
Too silver for a seam—
Or Butterflies, off Banks of Noon
Leap, plashless as they swim.

Emily Dickinson

'All things bright and beautiful'

All things bright and beautiful,
All creatures great and small,
All things wise and wonderful,
The Lord God made them all.

Each little flower that opens,
Each little bird that sings,
He made their glowing colours,
He made their tiny wings.

The rich man in his castle,
The poor man at his gate,
God made them, high or lowly,
And ordered their estate.

The purple-headed mountain,
The river running by,
The sunset, and the morning,
That brightens up the sky;

The cold wind in the winter,
The pleasant summer sun,
The ripe fruits in the garden,
He made them every one.

The tall trees in the greenwood,
The meadows where we play,
The rushes by the water,
We gather every day;—

He gave us eyes to see them,
And lips that we might tell,
How great is God Almighty,
Who has made all things well.

Cecil Frances Alexander

The Bluebell

The Bluebell is the sweetest flower
That waves in summer air:
Its blossoms have the mightiest power
To soothe my spirit's care.

There is a spell in purple heath
Too wildly, sadly dear;
The violet has a fragrant breath,
But fragrance will not cheer,

The trees are bare, the sun is cold,
And seldom, seldom seen;
The heavens have lost their zone of gold,
And earth her robe of green.

And ice upon the glancing stream
Has cast its sombre shade;
And distant hills and valleys seem
In frozen mist arrayed.

The Bluebell cannot charm me now,
The heath has lost its bloom;
The violets in the glen below,
They yield no sweet perfume.

But, though I mourn the sweet Bluebell,
'Tis better far away;
I know how fast my tears would swell
To see it smile to-day.

For, oh! when chill the sunbeams fall
Adown that dreary sky,
And gild yon dank and darkened wall
With transient brilliancy;

How do I weep, how do I pine
For the time of flowers to come,
And turn me from that fading shine,
To mourn the fields of home!

Emily Brontë

The Spider and the Fly

'Will you walk into my parlour?' said the Spider to the Fly,
'Tis the prettiest little parlour that ever you did spy;
The way into my parlour is up a winding stair,
And I've a many curious things to shew when you are there'
'Oh no, no,' said the little Fly, 'to ask me is in vain,
For who goes up your winding stair can ne'er come down
    again.'

'I'm sure you must be weary, dear, with soaring up so high;
Will you rest upon my little bed?' said the Spider to the Fly.
'There are pretty curtains drawn around; the sheets are fine
   and thin,
And if you like to rest awhile, I'll snugly tuck you in!'
'Oh no, no,' said the little Fly, 'for I've often heard it said,
They never, never wake again, who sleep upon your bed!'

Said the cunning Spider to the Fly, 'Dear friend what can I do,
To prove the warm affection I've always felt for you?
I have within my pantry, good store of all that's nice;
I'm sure you're very welcome – will you please to take a slice?'
'Oh no, no,' said the little Fly, 'kind Sir, that cannot be,
I've heard what's in your pantry, and I do not wish to see!'

'Sweet creature!' said the Spider, 'you're witty and you're wise,
How handsome are your gauzy wings, how brilliant are your
   eyes!
I've a little looking-glass upon my parlour shelf,
If you'll step in one moment, dear, you shall behold yourself.'
'I thank you, gentle sir,' she said, 'for what you're pleased to say,
And bidding you good morning now, I'll call another day.'

The Spider turned him round about, and went into his den,
For well he knew the silly Fly would soon come back again:
So he wove a subtle web, in a little corner sly,
And set his table ready, to dine upon the Fly.
Then he came out to his door again, and merrily did sing,
'Come hither, hither, pretty Fly, with the pearl and silver
   wing;
Your robes are green and purple – there's a crest upon your
   head;
Your eyes are like the diamond bright, but mine are dull as
   lead!'

Alas, alas! how very soon this silly little Fly,
Hearing his wily, flattering words, came slowly flitting by;
With buzzing wings she hung aloft, then near and nearer
   drew,
Thinking only of her brilliant eyes, and green and purple hue –
Thinking only of her crested head – poor foolish thing! At last,
Up jumped the cunning Spider, and fiercely held her fast.
He dragged her up his winding stair, into his dismal den,
Within his little parlour – but she ne'er came out again!

And now dear little children, who may this story read,
To idle, silly flattering words, I pray you ne'er give heed:
Unto an evil counsellor, close heart and ear and eye,
And take a lesson from this tale, of the Spider and the Fly.

Mary Howitt

The Rainbow

Boats sail on the rivers,
And ships sail on the seas;
But clouds that sail across the sky
Are prettier than these.

There are bridges on the rivers,
As pretty as you please;
But the bow that bridges heaven,
And overtops the trees,
And builds a road from earth to sky,
Is prettier far than these.

Christina Rossetti

Trees

I think that I shall never see
A poem lovely as a tree.

A tree whose hungry mouth is prest
Against the earth's sweet flowing breast;

A tree that looks at God all day,
And lifts her leafy arms to pray;

A tree that may in summer wear
A nest of robins in her hair;

Upon whose bosom snow has lain;
Who intimately lives with rain.

Poems are made by fools like me,
But only God can make a tree.

Joyce Kilmer

Nature

O Nature! I do not aspire
To be the highest in thy choir, –
To be a meteor in thy sky,
Or comet that may range on high;
Only a zephyr that may blow
Among the reeds by the river low;
Give me thy most privy place
Where to run my airy race.

In some withdrawn, unpublic mead
Let me sigh upon a reed,
Or in the woods, with leafy din,
Whisper the still evening in:
Some still work give me to do, –
Only – be it near to you!

For I'd rather be thy child
And pupil, in the forest wild,
Than be the king of men elsewhere,
And most sovereign slave of care;
To have one moment of thy dawn,
Than share the city's year forlorn.

Henry David Thoreau

'How doth the little crocodile'

How doth the little crocodile
Improve his shining tail,
And pour the waters of the Nile
On every golden scale!

How cheerfully he seems to grin
How neatly spreads his claws,
And welcomes little fishes in,
With gently smiling jaws!

Lewis Carroll

The Donkey

When fishes flew and forests walked
    And figs grew upon thorn,
Some moment when the moon was blood
    Then surely I was born.

With monstrous head and sickening cry
    And ears like errant wings,
The devil's walking parody
    On all four-footed things.

The tattered outlaw of the earth,
    Of ancient crooked will;
Starve, scourge, deride me: I am dumb,
    I keep my secret still.

Fools! For I also had my hour;
    One far fierce hour and sweet:
There was a shout about my ears,
    And palms before my feet.

G. K. Chesterton

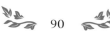

90

A Thunderstorm

A moment the wild swallows like a flight
Of withered gust-caught leaves, serenely high,
Toss in the windrack up the muttering sky.
The leaves hang still. Above the weird twilight,
The hurrying centres of the storm unite
And spreading with huge trunk and rolling fringe,
Each wheeled upon its own tremendous hinge,
Tower darkening on. And now from heaven's height,
With the long roar of elm-trees swept and swayed,
And pelted waters, on the vanished plain
Plunges the blast. Behind the wild white flash
That splits abroad the pealing thunder-crash,
Over bleared fields and gardens disarrayed,
Column on column comes the drenching rain.

Archibald Lampman

Four-Feet

I have done mostly what most men do,
And pushed it out of my mind;
But I can't forget, if I wanted to,
Four-Feet trotting behind.

Day after day, the whole day through –
Wherever my road inclined –
Four-Feet said, 'I am coming with you!'
And trotted along behind.

Now I must go by some other round, –
Which I shall never find –
Somewhere that does not carry the sound
Of Four-Feet trotting behind.

Rudyard Kipling

The Cat and the Moon

The cat went here and there
And the moon spun round like a top,
And the nearest kin of the moon,
The creeping cat, looked up.
Black Minnaloushe stared at the moon,
For, wander and wail as he would,
The pure cold light in the sky
Troubled his animal blood.
Minnaloushe runs in the grass
Lifting his delicate feet.
Do you dance, Minnaloushe, do you dance?
When two close kindred meet,

What better than call a dance?
Maybe the moon may learn,
Tired of that courtly fashion,
A new dance turn.
Minnaloushe creeps through the grass
From moonlit place to place,
The sacred moon overhead
Has taken a new phase.
Does Minnaloushe know that his pupils
Will pass from change to change,
And that from round to crescent,
From crescent to round they range?
Minnaloushe creeps through the grass
Alone, important and wise,
And lifts to the changing moon
His changing eyes.

W. B. Yeats

On a Cat, Aging

He blinks upon the hearth-rug,
and yawns in deep content,
accepting all the comforts
that Providence has sent.

Louder he purrs, and louder,
in one glad hymn of praise
for all the night's adventures,
for quiet, restful days.

Life will go on for ever,
with all that cat can wish:
warmth and the glad procession
of fish and milk and fish.

Only – the thought disturbs him –
he's noticed once or twice,
the times are somehow breeding
a nimbler race of mice.

Alexander Gray

Magic, Fantasy
and Nonsense

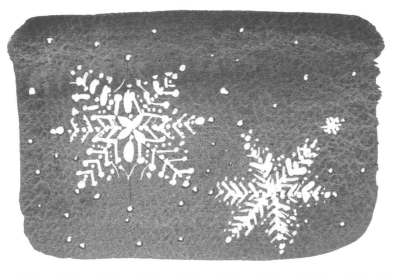

'Double, double toil and trouble'
from *Macbeth*

Double, double toil and trouble;
Fire burn and caldron bubble.
Fillet of a fenny snake,
In the caldron boil and bake;
Eye of newt and toe of frog,
Wool of bat and tongue of dog,
Adder's fork and blind-worm's sting,
Lizard's leg and howlet's wing,
For a charm of powerful trouble,
Like a hell-broth boil and bubble.

Double, double toil and trouble;
Fire burn and caldron bubble.
Cool it with a baboon's blood,
Then the charm is firm and good.

William Shakespeare

Ariel's Song from *The Tempest*

Come unto these yellow sands,
    And then take hands:
Curtsied when you have, and kiss'd
    The wild waves whist,
Foot it featly here and there;
And, sweet sprites, the burthen bear.
    Hark, hark!
Bow-wow.
    The watch-dogs bark.
Bow-wow.
    Hark, hark! I hear
    The strain of strutting chanticleer
    Cry, Cock-a-diddle-dow.

Full fathom five thy father lies;
    Of his bones are coral made;
Those are pearls that were his eyes:
    Nothing of him that doth fade,
But doth suffer a sea-change
Into something rich and strange.
Sea-nymphs hourly ring his knell:
        Ding-dong.
Hark! now I hear them—Ding-dong, bell.

William Shakespeare

97

Kubla Khan

In Xanadu did Kubla Khan
A stately pleasure-dome decree:
Where Alph, the sacred river, ran
Through caverns measureless to man
  Down to a sunless sea.
So twice five miles of fertile ground
With walls and towers were girdled round;
And there were gardens bright with sinuous rills,
Where blossomed many an incense-bearing tree;
And here were forests ancient as the hills,
Enfolding sunny spots of greenery.

But oh! that deep romantic chasm which slanted
Down the green hill athwart a cedarn cover!
A savage place! as holy and enchanted
As e'er beneath a waning moon was haunted
By woman wailing for her demon-lover!
And from this chasm, with ceaseless turmoil seething,
As if this earth in fast thick pants were breathing,
A mighty fountain momently was forced:
Amid whose swift half-intermitted burst
Huge fragments vaulted like rebounding hail,
Or chaffy grain beneath the thresher's flail:
And mid these dancing rocks at once and ever
It flung up momently the sacred river.
Five miles meandering with a mazy motion
Through wood and dale the sacred river ran,
Then reached the caverns measureless to man,
And sank in tumult to a lifeless ocean;

And 'mid this tumult Kubla heard from far
Ancestral voices prophesying war!
  The shadow of the dome of pleasure
  Floated midway on the waves;
  Where was heard the mingled measure
  From the fountain and the caves.
It was a miracle of rare device,
A sunny pleasure-dome with caves of ice!

  A damsel with a dulcimer
  In a vision once I saw:
  It was an Abyssinian maid
  And on her dulcimer she played,
  Singing of Mount Abora.
  Could I revive within me
  Her symphony and song,
  To such a deep delight 'twould win me,
That with music loud and long,
I would build that dome in air,
That sunny dome! those caves of ice!
And all who heard should see them there,
And all should cry, Beware! Beware!
His flashing eyes, his floating hair!
Weave a circle round him thrice,
And close your eyes with holy dread
For he on honey-dew hath fed,
And drunk the milk of Paradise.

Samuel Taylor Coleridge

Jabberwocky

'Twas brillig, and the slithy toves
    Did gyre and gimble in the wabe:
All mimsy were the borogoves,
    And the mome raths outgrabe.

'Beware the Jabberwock, my son!
    The jaws that bite, the claws that catch!
Beware the Jubjub bird, and shun
    The frumious Bandersnatch!'

He took his vorpal sword in hand;
    Long time the manxome foe he sought—
So rested he by the Tumtum tree
    And stood awhile in thought.

And, as in uffish thought he stood,
    The Jabberwock, with eyes of flame,
Came whiffling through the tulgey wood,
    And burbled as it came!

One, two! One, two! And through and through
    The vorpal blade went snicker-snack!
He left it dead, and with its head
    He went galumphing back.

'And hast thou slain the Jabberwock?
    Come to my arms, my beamish boy!
O frabjous day! Callooh! Callay!'
    He chortled in his joy.

'Twas brillig, and the slithy toves
    Did gyre and gimble in the wabe:
All mimsy were the borogoves,
    And the mome raths outgrabe.

Lewis Carroll

100

The Little Elf-Man

I met a little Elf-man once
Down where the lilies blow.
I asked him why he was so small,
And, why he didn't grow.

He slightly frowned, and with his eye
He looked me through and through.
'I'm just as big for me,' said he,
'As you are big for you!'

J. K. Bangs

The Sleepy Giant

My age is three hundred and seventy-two,
And I think, with the deepest regret,
How I used to pick up and voraciously chew
The dear little boys whom I met.

I've eaten them raw, in their holiday suits;
I've eaten them curried with rice;
I've eaten them baked, in their jackets and boots,
And found them exceedingly nice.

But now that my jaws are too weak for such fare,
I think it exceedingly rude
To do such a thing, when I'm quite well aware
Little boys do not like to be chewed.

And so I contentedly live upon eels,
And try to do nothing amiss,
And I pass all the time I can spare from my meals
In innocent slumber—like this.

Charles E. Carryl

Dream Land

Where sunless rivers weep
Their waves into the deep,
She sleeps a charmed sleep:
    Awake her not.
Led by a single star,
She came from very far
To seek where shadows are
    Her pleasant lot.

She left the rosy morn,
She left the fields of corn,
For twilight cold and lorn
    And water springs.
Through sleep, as through a veil,
She sees the sky look pale,
And hears the nightingale
    That sadly sings.

Rest, rest, a perfect rest
Shed over brow and breast;
Her face is toward the west,
    The purple land.
She cannot see the grain
Ripening on hill and plain;
She cannot feel the rain
    Upon her hand.

Rest, rest, for evermore
Upon a mossy shore;
Rest, rest at the heart's core
    Till time shall cease:
Sleep that no pain shall wake;
Night that no morn shall break
Till joy shall overtake
    Her perfect peace.

Christina Rossetti

Eldorado

Gaily bedight,
  A gallant knight,
In sunshine and in shadow,
  Had journeyed long,
  Singing a song,
In search of Eldorado.

But he grew old—
  This knight so bold—
And o'er his heart a shadow—
  Fell as he found
  No spot of ground
That looked like Eldorado.

And, as his strength
  Failed him at length,
He met a pilgrim shadow—
  'Shadow,' said he,
  'Where can it be—
This land of Eldorado?'

'Over the Mountains
Of the Moon,
Down the Valley of the Shadow,
Ride, boldly ride,'
The shade replied,—
'If you seek for Eldorado!'

Edgar Allan Poe

The Stolen Child

Where dips the rocky highland
Of Sleuth Wood in the lake,
There lies a leafy island
Where flapping herons wake
The drowsy water rats;
There we've hid our faery vats,
Full of berries
And of reddest stolen cherries.
Come away, O human child!
To the waters and the wild
With a faery, hand in hand,
For the world's more full of weeping than you can
understand.

Where the wave of moonlight glosses
The dim gray sands with light,
Far off by furthest Rosses
We foot it all the night,
Weaving olden dances
Mingling hands and mingling glances
Till the moon has taken flight;

104

To and fro we leap
And chase the frothy bubbles,
While the world is full of troubles
And anxious in its sleep.
Come away, O human child!
To the waters and the wild
With a faery, hand in hand,
For the world's more full of weeping than you can
  understand.

Where the wandering water gushes
From the hills above Glen-Car,
In pools among the rushes
That scarce could bathe a star,
We seek for slumbering trout
And whispering in their ears
Give them unquiet dreams;
Leaning softly out
From ferns that drop their tears
Over the young streams.
Come away, O human child!
To the waters and the wild
With a faery, hand in hand,
For the world's more full of weeping than you can
  understand.

Away with us he's going,
The solemn-eyed:
He'll hear no more the lowing
Of the calves on the warm hillside
Or the kettle on the hob
Sing peace into his breast,
Or see the brown mice bob

Round and round the oatmeal chest.
For he comes, the human child,
To the waters and the wild
With a faery, hand in hand,
For the world's more full of weeping than he can
    understand.

W. B. Yeats

The Owl and the Pussycat

I   The Owl and the Pussy-cat went to sea
      In a beautiful pea-green boat,
    They took some honey, and plenty of money,
      Wrapped up in a five-pound note.
    The Owl looked up to the stars above,
      And sang to a small guitar,
    "O lovely Pussy! O Pussy, my love,
      What a beautiful Pussy you are,
          You are,
          You are!
    What a beautiful Pussy you are!"

II   Pussy said to the Owl, "You elegant fowl!
      How charmingly sweet you sing!
    O let us be married! too long we have tarried:
      But what shall we do for a ring?"
    They sailed away, for a year and a day,
      To the land where the Bong-Tree grows
    And there in a wood a Piggy-wig stood
      With a ring at the end of his nose,
          His nose,
          His nose,
    With a ring at the end of his nose.

III   "Dear Pig, are you willing to sell for one shilling
      Your ring?" Said the Piggy, "I will."
    So they took it away, and were married next day
      By the Turkey who lives on the hill.
    They dined on mince, and slices of quince,
      Which they ate with a runcible spoon;

And hand in hand, on the edge of the sand,
   They danced by the light of the moon,
      The moon,
      The moon,
They danced by the light of the moon.

Edward Lear

The Fairies

Up the airy mountain,
   Down the rushy glen,
We daren't go a-hunting
   For fear of little men;
Wee folk, good folk,
   Trooping all together;
Green jacket, red cap,
   And white owl's feather!

Down along the rocky shore
   Some make their home,
They live on crispy pancakes
   Of yellow tide-foam;
Some in the reeds
   Of the black mountain lake,
With frogs for their watch-dogs,
   All night awake.

High on the hill-top
   The old King sits;
He is now so old and gray
   He's nigh lost his wits.
With a bridge of white mist
   Columbkill he crosses,
On his stately journeys
   From Slieveleague to Rosses;
Or going up with music
   On cold starry nights
To sup with the Queen
   Of the gay Northern Lights.

They stole little Bridget
    For seven years long;
When she came down again
    Her friends were all gone.
They took her lightly back,
    Between the night and morrow,
They thought that she was fast asleep,
    But she was dead with sorrow.
They have kept her ever since
    Deep within the lake,
On a bed of flag-leaves,
    Watching till she wake.

By the craggy hill-side,
    Through the mosses bare,
They have planted thorn-trees
    For pleasure here and there.
If any man so daring
    As dig them up in spite,
He shall find their sharpest thorns
    In his bed at night.

Up the airy mountain,
    Down the rushy glen,
We daren't go a-hunting
    For fear of little men;
Wee folk, good folk,
    Trooping all together;
Green jacket, red cap,
    And white owl's feather!

William Allingham

The Duel

The gingham dog and the calico cat
Side by side on the table sat;
'Twas half-past twelve, and (what do you think!)
Nor one nor t'other had slept a wink!
  The old Dutch clock and the Chinese plate
  Appeared to know as sure as fate
There was going to be a terrible spat.
  (I wasn't there; I simply state
  What was told to me by the Chinese plate!)

The gingham dog went 'bow-wow-wow!'
And the calico cat replied 'mee-ow!'
The air was littered, an hour or so,
With bits of gingham and calico,
  While the old Dutch clock in the chimney-place
  Up with its hands before its face,
For it always dreaded a family row!
  (Never mind: I'm only telling you
  What the old Dutch clock declares is true!)

The Chinese plate looked very blue,
And wailed, 'Oh, dear! what shall we do!'
But the gingham dog and the calico cat
Wallowed this way and tumbled that,
  Employing every tooth and claw
  In the awfullest way you ever saw—
And, oh! how the gingham and calico flew!
  (Don't fancy I exaggerate—
  I got my news from the Chinese plate!)

Next morning where the two had sat
They found no trace of dog or cat;
And some folks think unto this day
That burglars stole that pair away!
  But the truth about the cat and pup
  Is this: they ate each other up!
Now what do you really think of that!
  (The old Dutch clock it told me so,
  And that is how I came to know.)

Eugene Field

Triolet

I wish I were a jelly fish
That cannot fall downstairs;
Of all the things I wish to wish
I wish I were a jellyfish
That hasn't any cares
And doesn't even have to wish
'I wish I were a jellyfish
That cannot fall downstairs.'

G. K. Chesterton

Travels and
Place

Lines Composed While Climbing the Left Ascent of Brockley Coomb

With many a pause and oft reverted eye
I climb the Coomb's ascent: sweet songsters near
Warble in shade their wild-wood melody:
Far off the unvarying Cuckoo soothes my ear.
Up scour the startling stragglers of the flock
That on green plots o'er precipices browse:
From the deep fissures of the naked rock
The Yew-tree bursts! Beneath its dark green boughs
('Mid which the May-thorn blends its blossoms white)
Where broad smooth stones jut out in mossy seats,
I rest: —and now have gained the topmost site.
Ah! what a luxury of landscape meets
My gaze! Proud towers, and Cots more dear to me,
Elm-shadowed Fields, and prospect-bounding Sea.
Deep sighs my lonely heart: I drop the tear:
Enchanting spot! O were my Sara here.

Samuel Taylor Coleridge

My Heart's in the Highlands

Farewell to the Highlands, farewell to the North,
The birth-place of Valour, the country of Worth;
Wherever I wander, wherever I rove,
The hills of the Highlands for ever I love.

My heart's in the Highlands, my heart is not here,
My heart's in the Highlands, a-chasing the deer;
Chasing the wild-deer, and following the roe,
My heart's in the Highlands, wherever I go.

Farewell to the mountains, high-cover'd with snow,
Farewell to the straths and green vallies below;
Farewell to the forests and wild-hanging woods,
Farewell to the torrents and loud-pouring floods.

My heart's in the Highlands, my heart is not here,
My heart's in the Highlands, a-chasing the deer;
Chasing the wild-deer, and following the roe,
My heart's in the Highlands, wherever I go.

Robert Burns

London

I wander thro' each charter'd street,
Near where the charter'd Thames does flow.
And mark in every face I meet
Marks of weakness, marks of woe.

In every cry of every Man,
In every Infant's cry of fear,
In every voice: in every ban,
The mind-forg'd manacles I hear

How the Chimney-sweepers cry
Every blackning Church appalls,
And the hapless Soldier's sigh
Runs in blood down Palace walls

But most thro' midnight streets I hear
How the youthful Harlot's curse
Blasts the new-born Infant's tear
And blights with plagues the Marriage hearse

William Blake

On First Looking into Chapman's Homer

Much have I travell'd in the realms of gold,
    And many goodly states and kingdoms seen;
    Round many western islands have I been
Which bards in fealty to Apollo hold.
Oft of one wide expanse had I been told
    That deep-brow'd Homer ruled as his demesne;
    Yet did I never breathe its pure serene
Till I heard Chapman speak out loud and bold:
Then felt I like some watcher of the skies
    When a new planet swims into his ken;
Or like stout Cortez when with eagle eyes
    He star'd at the Pacific—and all his men
Look'd at each other with a wild surmise—
    Silent, upon a peak in Darien.

John Keats

Ozymandias

I met a traveller from an antique land
Who said: Two vast and trunkless legs of stone
Stand in the desert. Near them on the sand,
Half sunk, a shatter'd visage lies, whose frown
And wrinkled lip and sneer of cold command
Tell that its sculptor well those passions read
Which yet survive, stamp'd on these lifeless things,
The hand that mock'd them and the heart that fed.

And on the pedestal these words appear:
'My name is Ozymandias, king of kings:
Look on my works, ye Mighty, and despair!'
Nothing beside remains: round the decay
Of that colossal wreck, boundless and bare,
The lone and level sands stretch far away.

Percy Bysshe Shelley

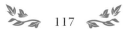

Home Thoughts, From Abroad

Oh, to be in England
Now that April's there,
And whoever wakes in England
Sees, some morning, unaware,
That the lowest boughs and the brushwood sheaf
Round the elm-tree bole are in tiny leaf,
While the chaffinch sings on the orchard bough
In England—now!

And after April, when May follows,
And the whitethroat builds, and all the swallows!
Hark, where my blossomed pear-tree in the hedge
Leans to the field and scatters on the clover
Blossoms and dewdrops—at the bent spray's edge—
That's the wise thrush; he sings each song twice over,
Lest you should think he never could recapture
The first fine careless rapture!
And though the fields look rough with hoary dew,
All will be gay when noontide wakes anew
The buttercups, the little children's dower
—Far brighter than this gaudy melon-flower!

Robert Browning

From a Railway Carriage

Faster than fairies, faster than witches,
Bridges and houses, hedges and ditches;
And charging along like troops in a battle
All through the meadows the horses and cattle:
All of the sights of the hill and the plain
Fly as thick as driving rain;
And ever again, in the wink of an eye,
Painted stations whistle by.
Here is a child who clambers and scrambles,
All by himself and gathering brambles;
Here is a tramp who stands and gazes;
And here is the green for stringing the daisies!
Here is a cart runaway in the road
Lumping along with man and load;
And here is a mill, and there is a river:
Each a glimpse and gone forever!

Robert Louis Stevenson

On Wenlock Edge

On Wenlock Edge the wood's in trouble;
    His forest fleece the Wrekin heaves;
The gale, it plies the saplings double,
    And thick on Severn snow the leaves.

'Twould blow like this through holt and hanger
    When Uricon the city stood:
'Tis the old wind in the old anger,
    But then it threshed another wood.
Then, 'twas before my time, the Roman
    At yonder heaving hill would stare:
The blood that warms an English yeoman,
    The thoughts that hurt him, they were there.

There, like the wind through woods in riot,
    Through him the gale of life blew high;
The tree of man was never quiet:
    Then 'twas the Roman, now 'tis I.

The gale, it plies the saplings double,
    It blows so hard, 'twill soon be gone:
To-day the Roman and his trouble
    Are ashes under Uricon.

A. E. Housman

The Engine

Into the gloom of the deep, dark night,
  With panting breath and a startled scream;
Swift as a bird in sudden flight
  Darts this creature of steel and steam.

Awful dangers are lurking nigh,
  Rocks and chasms are near the track,
But straight by the light of its great white eye
  It speeds through the shadows, dense and black.

Terrible thoughts and fierce desires
  Trouble its mad heart many an hour,
Where burn and smoulder the hidden fires,
  Coupled ever with might and power.

It hates, as a wild horse hates the rein,
  The narrow track by vale and hill;
And shrieks with a cry of startled pain,
  And longs to follow its own wild will.

Ella Wheeler Wilcox

The Night Journey

Hands and lit faces eddy to a line;
  The dazed last minutes click; the clamour dies.
Beyond the great-swung arc o' the roof, divine,
  Night, smoky-scarv'd, with thousand coloured eyes

Glares the imperious mystery of the way.
  Thirsty for dark, you feel the long-limbed train
Throb, stretch, thrill motion, slide, pull out and sway,
  Strain for the far, pause, draw to strength again…

As a man, caught by some great hour, will rise,
  Slow-limbed, to meet the light or find his love;
And, breathing long, with staring sightless eyes,
  Hands out, head back, agape and silent, move

Sure as a flood, smooth as a vast wind blowing;
  And, gathering power and purpose as he goes,
Unstumbling, unreluctant, strong, unknowing,
  Borne by a will not his, that lifts, that grows,

Sweep out to darkness, triumphing in his goal,
  Out of the fire, out of the little room…
—There is an end appointed, O my soul!
  Crimson and green the signals burn; the gloom

Is hung with steam's far-blowing livid streamers.
  Lost into God, as lights in light, we fly,
Grown one with will, end-drunken huddled dreamers.
  The white lights roar. The sounds of the world die.

And lips and laughter are forgotten things.
  Speed sharpens; grows. Into the night, and on,
The strength and splendour of our purpose swings.
  The lamps fade; and the stars. We are alone.

Rupert Brooke

Poppies on Ludlow Castle

Through halls of vanished pleasure,
And hold of vanished power,
And crypt of faith forgotten,
A came to Ludlow tower.

A-top of arch and stairway,
Of crypt and donjan cell,
Of council hall, and chamber,
Of wall, and ditch, and well,

High over grated turrets
Where clinging ivies run,
A thousand scarlet poppies
Enticed the rising sun,

Upon the topmost turret,
With death and damp below,–
Three hundred years of spoilage,–
The crimson poppies grow.

This hall it was that bred him,
These hills that knew him brave,
The gentlest English singer
That fills an English grave.

How have they heart to blossom
So cruel and gay and red,
When beauty so hath perished
And valour so hath sped?

When knights so fair are rotten,
And captains true asleep,
And singing lips are dust-stopped
Six English earth-feet deep?

When ages old remind me
How much hath gone for naught,
What wretched ghost remaineth
Of all that flesh hath wrought;

Of love and song and warring,
Of adventure and play,
Of art and comely building,
Of faith and form and fray—

I'll mind the flowers of pleasure,
Of short-lived youth and sleep,
That drunk the sunny weather
A-top of Ludlow keep.

Willa Cather

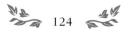

Adlestrop

Yes, I remember Adlestrop –
The name, because one afternoon
Of heat the express-train drew up there
Unwontedly. It was late June.

The steam hissed. Someone cleared his throat.
No one left and no one came
On the bare platform. What I saw
Was Adlestrop – only the name

And willows, willow-herb, and grass,
And meadowsweet, and haycocks dry,
No whit less still and lonely fair
Than the high cloudlets in the sky.

And for that minute a blackbird sang
Close by, and round him, mistier,
Farther and farther, all the birds
Of Oxfordshire and Gloucestershire.

Edward Thomas

Ballade of an Omnibus

Some men to carriages aspire;
On some the costly hansoms wait;
Some seek a fly, on job or hire;
Some mount the trotting steed, elate.
I envy not the rich and great,
A wandering minstrel, poor and free,
I am contented with my fate –
An omnibus suffices me.

In winter days of rain and mire
I find within a corner strait;
The 'busmen know me and my lyre
From Brompton to the Bull-and-Gate.
When summer comes, I mount in state
The topmost summit, whence I see
Crœsus look up, compassionate –
An omnibus suffices me.

I mark, untroubled by desire,
Lucullus' phaeton and its freight.
The scene whereof I cannot tire,
The human tale of love and hate,
The city pageant, early and late
Unfolds itself, rolls by, to be
A pleasure deep and delicate.
An omnibus suffices me.

Princess, your splendour you require,
I, my simplicity; agree
Neither to rate lower nor higher.
An omnibus suffices me.

Amy Levy

'There is no Frigate like a Book'

There is no Frigate like a Book
To take us Lands away,
Nor any Coursers like a Page
Of prancing Poetry –
This Traverse may the poorest take
Without oppress of Toll –
How frugal is the Chariot
That bears a Human soul.

Emily Dickinson

I Hear America Singing

I hear America singing, the varied carols I hear,
Those of mechanics, each one singing his as it should be
    blithe and strong,
The carpenter singing his as he measures his plank or beam,
The mason singing his as he makes ready for work, or leaves
    off work,
The boatman singing what belongs to him in his boat, the
    deckhand singing on the steamboat deck,
The shoemaker singing as he sits on his bench, the hatter
    singing as he stands,
The wood-cutter's song, the ploughboy's on his way in the
    morning, or at noon intermission or at sundown,
The delicious singing of the mother, or of the young wife at
    work, or of the girl sewing or washing,
Each singing what belongs to him or her and to none else,
The day what belongs to the day—at night the party of young
    fellows, robust, friendly,
Singing with open mouths their strong melodious songs.

Walt Whitman

The Spell of the Yukon

I wanted the gold, and I sought it;
　　I scrabbled and mucked like a slave.
Was it famine or scurvy—I fought it;
　　I hurled my youth into a grave.
I wanted the gold, and I got it—
　　Came out with a fortune last fall,—
Yet somehow life's not what I thought it,
　　And somehow the gold isn't all.

No! There's the land. (Have you seen it?)
　　It's the cussedest land that I know,
From the big, dizzy mountains that screen it
　　To the deep, deathlike valleys below.
Some say God was tired when He made it;
　　Some say it's a fine land to shun;
Maybe; but there's some as would trade it
　　For no land on earth—and I'm one.

You come to get rich (damned good reason);
　　You feel like an exile at first;
You hate it like hell for a season,
　　And then you are worse than the worst.
It grips you like some kinds of sinning;
　　It twists you from foe to a friend;
It seems it's been since the beginning;
　　It seems it will be to the end.

I've stood in some mighty-mouthed hollow
    That's plumb-full of hush to the brim;
I've watched the big, husky sun wallow
    In crimson and gold, and grow dim,
Till the moon set the pearly peaks gleaming,
    And the stars tumbled out, neck and crop;
And I've thought that I surely was dreaming,
    With the peace o' the world piled on top.

The summer—no sweeter was ever;
    The sunshiny woods all athrill;
The grayling aleap in the river,
    The bighorn asleep on the hill.
The strong life that never knows harness;
    The wilds where the caribou call;
The freshness, the freedom, the farness—
    O God! how I'm stuck on it all.

The winter! the brightness that blinds you,
    The white land locked tight as a drum,
The cold fear that follows and finds you,
    The silence that bludgeons you dumb.
The snows that are older than history,
    The woods where the weird shadows slant;
The stillness, the moonlight, the mystery,
    I've bade 'em good-by—but I can't.

There's a land where the mountains are nameless,
    And the rivers all run God knows where;
There are lives that are erring and aimless,
    And deaths that just hang by a hair;

There are hardships that nobody reckons;
  There are valleys unpeopled and still;
There's a land—oh, it beckons and beckons,
  And I want to go back—and I will.

They're making my money diminish;
  I'm sick of the taste of champagne.
Thank God! when I'm skinned to a finish
  I'll pike to the Yukon again.
I'll fight—and you bet it's no sham-fight;
  It's hell!—but I've been there before;
And it's better than this by a damsite—
  So me for the Yukon once more.

There's gold, and it's haunting and haunting;
  It's luring me on as of old;
Yet it isn't the gold that I'm wanting
  So much as just finding the gold.
It's the great, big, broad land 'way up yonder,
  It's the forests where silence has lease;
It's the beauty that thrills me with wonder,
  It's the stillness that fills me with peace.

Robert Service

Autumn at Taos

Over the rounded sides of
   the Rockies, the aspens of autumn,
The aspens of autumn,
Like yellow hair of a tigress brindled with pines.

Down on my hearth-rug of desert, sage of the mesa,
An ash-grey pelt
Of wolf all hairy and level, a wolf's wild pelt.

Trot-trot to the mottled foot-hills, cedar-mottled and pinion;
Did you ever see an otter?
Silvery-sided, fish-fanged, fierce-faced, whiskered, mottled.

When I trot my little pony through the aspen-trees of the
   canyon,
Behold me trotting at ease betwixt the slopes of the golden
Great and glistening-feathered legs of the hawk of Horus;
The golden hawk of Horus
Astride above me.

But under the pines
I go slowly
As under the hairy belly of a great black bear.

Glad to emerge and look back
On the yellow, pointed aspen-trees laid one on another like
   feathers,
Feather over feather on the breast of the great and golden
Hawk as I say of Horus.

Pleased to be out in the sage and the pine fish-dotted
   foothills,
Past the otter's whiskers,
On to the fur of the wolf-pelt that strews the plain.

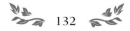

And then to look back to the rounded sides of the squatting
    Rockies.
Tigress brindled with aspen,
Jaguar-splashed, puma-yellow, leopard-livid slopes of
    America.

Make big eyes, little pony,
At all these skins of wild beasts;
They won't hurt you.

Fangs and claws and talons and beaks and hawk-eyes
Are nerveless just now.
So be easy.

                                        D. H. Lawrence

The Lake Isle of Innisfree

I will arise and go now, and go to Innisfree,
And a small cabin build there, of clay and wattles made:
Nine bean-rows will I have there, a hive for the honey-bee;
And live alone in the bee-loud glade.

And I shall have some peace there, for peace comes dropping
    slow,
Dropping from the veils of the morning to where the cricket
    sings;
There midnight's all a glimmer, and noon a purple glow,
And evening full of the linnet's wings.

I will arise and go now, for always night and day
I hear lake water lapping with low sounds by the shore;
While I stand on the roadway, or on the pavements grey,
I hear it in the deep heart's core.

W. B. Yeats

On the Mississippi

Through wild and tangled forests
The broad, unhasting river flows—
Spotted with rain-drops, gray with night;
Upon its curving breast there goes
A lonely steamboat's larboard light,
A blood-red star against the shadowy oaks;
Noiseless as a ghost, through greenish gleam
Of fire-flies, before the boat's wild scream—
A heron flaps away
Like silence taking flight.

Hamlin Garland

The Listeners

'Is there anybody there?' said the Traveller,
  Knocking on the moonlit door;
And his horse in the silence champed the grasses
  Of the forest's ferny floor:
And a bird flew up out of the turret,
  Above the Traveller's head:
And he smote upon the door again a second time;
  'Is there anybody there?' he said.
But no one descended to the Traveller;
  No head from the leaf-fringed sill
Leaned over and looked into his grey eyes,
  Where he stood perplexed and still.
But only a host of phantom listeners
  That dwelt in the lone house then
Stood listening in the quiet of the moonlight
  To that voice from the world of men:
Stood thronging the faint moonbeams on the dark stair,
  That goes down to the empty hall,
Hearkening in an air stirred and shaken
  By the lonely Traveller's call.

And he felt in his heart their strangeness,
  Their stillness answering his cry,
While his horse moved, cropping the dark turf,
  'Neath the starred and leafy sky;
For he suddenly smote on the door, even
  Louder, and lifted his head:—
'Tell them I came, and no one answered,
  That I kept my word,' he said.
Never the least stir made the listeners,
  Though every word he spake
Fell echoing through the shadowiness of the still house
  From the one man left awake:
Ay, they heard his foot upon the stirrup,
  And the sound of iron on stone,
And how the silence surged softly backward,
  When the plunging hoofs were gone.

Walter de la Mare

Reflections
and Musings

Shadows in the Water

In unexperienced infancy
Many a sweet mistake doth lie:
Mistake though false, intending true;
A seeming somewhat more than view;
    That doth instruct the mind
    In things that lie behind,
And many secrets to us show
Which afterwards we come to know.

Thus did I by the water's brink
Another world beneath me think;
And while the lofty spacious skies
Reversèd there, abused mine eyes,
    I fancied other feet
    Came mine to touch or meet;
As by some puddle I did play
Another world within it lay.

Beneath the water people drowned,
Yet with another heaven crowned,
In spacious regions seemed to go
As freely moving to and fro:
    In bright and open space
    I saw their very face;
Eyes, hands, and feet they had like mine;
Another sun did with them shine.

'Twas strange that people there should walk,
And yet I could not hear them talk:
That through a little watery chink,
Which one dry ox or horse might drink,
    We other worlds should see,
    Yet not admitted be;
And other confines there behold
Of light and darkness, heat and cold.

I called them oft, but called in vain;
No speeches we could entertain:
Yet did I there expect to find
Some other world, to please my mind.
    I plainly saw by these
    A new antipodes,
Whom, though they were so plainly seen,
A film kept off that stood between.

By walking men's reversèd feet
I chanced another world to meet;
Though it did not to view exceed
A phantom, 'tis a world indeed;
    Where skies beneath us shine,
    And earth by art divine
Another face presents below,
Where people's feet against ours go.

Within the regions of the air,
Compassed about with heavens fair,
Great tracts of land there may be found
Enriched with fields and fertile ground;
    Where many numerous hosts
    In those far distant coasts,
For other great and glorious ends
Inhabit, my yet unknown friends.

O ye that stand upon the brink,
Whom I so near me through the chink
With wonder see: what faces there,
Whose feet, whose bodies, do ye wear?
    I my companions see
    In you another me.
They seemèd others, but are we;
Our second selves these shadows be.

Look how far off those lower skies
Extend themselves! scarce with mine eyes
I can them reach. O ye my friends,
What secret borders on those ends?
    Are lofty heavens hurled
    'Bout your inferior world?
Are yet the representatives
Of other peoples' distant lives?

Of all the playmates which I knew
That here I do the image view
In other selves, what can it mean?
But that below the purling stream
    Some unknown joys there be
    Laid up in store for me;
To which I shall, when that thin skin
Is broken, be admitted in.

Thomas Traherne

Light Shining Out of Darkness

God moves in a mysterious way,
    His wonders to perform;
He plants his footsteps in the sea,
    And rides upon the storm.

Deep in unfathomable mines
    Of never-failing skill,
He treasures up his bright designs,
    And works his sov'reign will.

Ye fearful saints, fresh courage take,
    The clouds ye so much dread
Are big with mercy, and shall break
    In blessings on your head.

Judge not the Lord by feeble sense,
    But trust him for his grace;
Behind a frowning providence
    He hides a smiling face.

His purposes will ripen fast,
    Unfolding ev'ry hour;
The bud may have a bitter taste,
    But sweet will be the flow'r.

Blind unbelief is sure to err,
    And scan his work in vain;
God is his own interpreter,
    And he will make it plain.

William Cowper

Song from *Pippa Passes*

The year's at the spring,
And day's at the morn;
Morning's at seven;
The hill-side's dew-pearl'd;
The lark's on the wing;
The snail's on the thorn;
God's in His heaven—
All's right with the world.

Robert Browning

Jerusalem

And did those feet in ancient time
Walk upon England's mountains green:
And was the holy Lamb of God,
On England's pleasant pastures seen!

And did the Countenance Divine,
Shine forth upon our clouded hills?
And was Jerusalem builded here,
Among these dark Satanic Mills?

Bring me my Bow of burning gold:
Bring me my arrows of desire:
Bring me my Spear: O clouds unfold!
Bring me my Chariot of fire!

I will not cease from Mental Fight,
Nor shall my sword sleep in my hand:
Till we have built Jerusalem,
In England's green and pleasant Land.

William Blake

'A slumber did my spirit seal'

A slumber did my spirit seal;
 I had no human fears:
She seem'd a thing that could not feel
 The touch of earthly years.

No motion has she now, no force;
 She neither hears nor sees;
Roll'd round in earth's diurnal course
 With rocks, and stones, and trees.

William Wordsworth

'I'm happiest when most away'

I'm happiest when most away
I can bear my soul from its home of clay
On a windy night when the moon is bright
And the eye can wander through worlds of light—

When I am not and none beside—
Nor earth nor sea nor cloudless sky—
But only spirit wandering wide
Through infinite immensity.

Emily Brontë

"Hope' is the thing with feathers'

'Hope' is the thing with feathers –
That perches in the soul –
And sings the tune without the words –
And never stops – at all –

And sweetest – in the Gale – is heard –
And sore must be the storm –
That could abash the little Bird
That kept so many warm –

I've heard it in the chillest land –
And on the strangest Sea –
Yet – never – in Extremity,
It asked a crumb – of me.

Emily Dickinson

I Am

I am—yet what I am none cares or knows;
My friends forsake me like a memory lost:
I am the self-consumer of my woes—
They rise and vanish in oblivious host,
Like shadows in love's frenzied stifled throes
And yet I am, and live—like vapours tossed

Into the nothingness of scorn and noise,
Into the living sea of waking dreams,
Where there is neither sense of life or joys,
But the vast shipwreck of my life's esteems;
Even the dearest that I loved the best
Are strange—nay, rather, stranger than the rest.

I long for scenes where man hath never trod
A place where woman never smiled or wept
There to abide with my Creator, God,
And sleep as I in childhood sweetly slept,
Untroubling and untroubled where I lie
The grass below—above the vaulted sky.

John Clare

Pied Beauty

Glory be to God for dappled things—
  For skies of couple-colour as a brinded cow;
    For rose-moles all in stipple upon trout that swim;
Fresh-firecoal chestnut-falls; finches' wings;
  Landscape plotted and pieced—fold, fallow, and plough;
    And áll trádes, their gear and tackle and trim.

All things counter, original, spare, strange;
   Whatever is fickle, freckled (who knows how?)
     With swift, slow; sweet, sour; adazzle, dim;
He fathers-forth whose beauty is past change:
     Praise him.

Gerard Manley Hopkins

Up-hill

Does the road wind up-hill all the way?
   Yes, to the very end.
Will the day's journey take the whole long day?
   From morn to night, my friend.

But is there for the night a resting-place?
   A roof for when the slow dark hours begin.
May not the darkness hide it from my face?
   You cannot miss that inn.

Shall I meet other wayfarers at night?
   Those who have gone before.
Then must I knock, or call when just in sight?
   They will not keep you standing at that door.

Shall I find comfort, travel-sore and weak?
   Of labour you shall find the sum.
Will there be beds for me and all who seek?
   Yea, beds for all who come.

Christina Rossetti

Crossing the Bar

Sunset and evening star,
    And one clear call for me!
And may there be no moaning of the bar,
    When I put out to sea,
But such a tide as moving seems asleep,
    Too full for sound and foam,
When that which drew from out the boundless deep
    Turns again home.

Twilight and evening bell,
    And after that the dark!
And may there be no sadness or farewell,
    When I embark;

For tho' from out our bourne of Time and Place
    The flood may bear me far,
I hope to see my Pilot face to face
    When I have crost the bar.

Alfred, Lord Tennyson

Dover Beach

The sea is calm tonight.
The tide is full, the moon lies fair
Upon the straits; on the French coast the light
Gleams and is gone; the cliffs of England stand,
Glimmering and vast, out in the tranquil bay.
Come to the window, sweet is the night-air!
Only, from the long line of spray
Where the sea meets the moon-blanched land,
Listen! you hear the grating roar
Of pebbles which the waves draw back, and fling,
At their return, up the high strand,
Begin, and cease, and then again begin,
With tremulous cadence slow, and bring
The eternal note of sadness in.

Sophocles long ago
Heard it on the Ægean, and it brought
Into his mind the turbid ebb and flow
Of human misery; we
Find also in the sound a thought,
Hearing it by this distant northern sea.

The Sea of Faith
Was once, too, at the full, and round earth's shore
Lay like the folds of a bright girdle furled.
But now I only hear
Its melancholy, long, withdrawing roar,
Retreating, to the breath
Of the night-wind, down the vast edges drear
And naked shingles of the world.

Ah, love, let us be true
To one another! for the world, which seems
To lie before us like a land of dreams,
So various, so beautiful, so new,
Hath really neither joy, nor love, nor light,
Nor certitude, nor peace, nor help for pain;
And we are here as on a darkling plain
Swept with confused alarms of struggle and flight,
Where ignorant armies clash by night.

Matthew Arnold

Leisure

What is this life if, full of care,
We have no time to stand and stare?—

No time to stand beneath the boughs,
And stare as long as sheep and cows:

No time to see, when woods we pass,
Where squirrels hide their nuts in grass:

No time to see, in broad daylight,
Streams full of stars, like skies at night:

No time to turn at Beauty's glance,
And watch her feet, how they can dance:

No time to wait till her mouth can
Enrich that smile her eyes began?

A poor life this if, full of care,
We have no time to stand and stare.

W. H. Davies

I Sit and Look Out

I sit and look out upon all the sorrows of the world, and
  upon all oppression and shame;
I hear secret convulsive sobs from young men, at anguish
  with themselves, remorseful after deeds done;
I see, in low life, the mother misused by her children,
  dying, neglected, gaunt, desperate;
I see the wife misused by her husband—I see the
  treacherous seducer of young women;
I mark the ranklings of jealousy and unrequited love,
  attempted to be hid—I see these sights on the earth;
I see the workings of battle, pestilence, tyranny—I see
  martyrs and prisoners;
I observe a famine at sea—I observe the sailors casting
  lots who shall be kill'd, to preserve the lives of the rest;
I observe the slights and degradations cast by arrogant
  persons upon laborers, the poor, and upon negroes, and
  the like;
All these—All the meanness and agony without end,
  I sitting, look out upon,
See, hear, and am silent.

Walt Whitman

Invictus

Out of the night that covers me,
　　Black as the pit from pole to pole,
I thank whatever gods may be
　　For my unconquerable soul.

In the fell clutch of circumstance
　　I have not winced nor cried aloud.
Under the bludgeonings of chance
　　My head is bloody, but unbowed.

Beyond this place of wrath and tears
　　Looms but the Horror of the shade,
And yet the menace of the years
　　Finds and shall find me unafraid.

It matters not how strait the gate,
　　How charged with punishments the scroll,
I am the master of my fate,
　　I am the captain of my soul.

William Ernest Henley

If

If you can keep your head when all about you
　Are losing theirs and blaming it on you,
If you can trust yourself when all men doubt you,
　But make allowance for their doubting too;
If you can wait and not be tired by waiting,
　Or being lied about, don't deal in lies,
Or being hated, don't give way to hating,
　And yet don't look too good, nor talk too wise:

If you can dream—and not make dreams your master;
  If you can think—and not make thoughts your aim;
If you can meet with Triumph and Disaster
  And treat those two impostors just the same;
If you can bear to hear the truth you've spoken
  Twisted by knaves to make a trap for fools,
Or watch the things you gave your life to, broken,
  And stoop and build 'em up with worn-out tools:

If you can make one heap of all your winnings
  And risk it on one turn of pitch-and-toss,
And lose, and start again at your beginnings
  And never breathe a word about your loss;
If you can force your heart and nerve and sinew
  To serve your turn long after they are gone,
And so hold on when there is nothing in you
  Except the Will which says to them: 'Hold on!'

If you can talk with crowds and keep your virtue,
  Or walk with Kings—nor lose the common touch,
If neither foes nor loving friends can hurt you,
  If all men count with you, but none too much;
If you can fill the unforgiving minute
  With sixty seconds' worth of distance run,
Yours is the Earth and everything that's in it,
  And—which is more—you'll be a Man, my son!

Rudyard Kipling

Of Many Worlds in this World

Just like as in a nest of boxes round,
Degrees of sizes in each box are found:
So, in this world, may many others be
Thinner and less, and less still by degree:
Although they are not subject to our sense,
A world may be no bigger than two-pence.
Nature is curious, and such works may shape,
Which our dull senses easily escape:
For creatures, small as atoms, may there be,
If every one a creature's figure bear.
If atoms four, a world can make, then see
What several worlds might in an ear-ring be:
For, millions of those atoms may be in
The head of one small, little, single pin.
And if thus small, then ladies may well wear
A world of worlds, as pendants in each ear.

Margaret Cavendish

Little Things

Little drops of water,
Little grains of sand,
Make the mighty ocean
And the pleasant land.

Thus the little minutes,
Humble though they be,
Make the mighty ages
Of eternity.

Ebenezer Cobham Brewer

War and Peace

Peace

My Soul, there is a country
    Afar beyond the stars,
Where stands a winged sentry
    All skilful in the wars;
There, above noise and danger
    Sweet Peace sits, crown'd with smiles,
And One born in a manger
    Commands the beauteous files.
He is thy gracious friend
    And (O my Soul awake!)
Did in pure love descend,
    To die here for thy sake.
If thou canst get but thither,
    There grows the flow'r of peace,
The rose that cannot wither,
    Thy fortress, and thy ease.
Leave then thy foolish ranges,
    For none can thee secure,
But One, who never changes,
    Thy God, thy life, thy cure.

Henry Vaughan

To Lucasta, Going to the Wars

Tell me not (Sweet) I am unkind,
    That from the nunnery
Of thy chaste breast and quiet mind
    To war and arms I fly.

True, a new mistress now I chase,
    The first foe in the field;
And with a stronger faith embrace
    A sword, a horse, a shield.

Yet this inconstancy is such
    As you too shall adore;
I could not love thee (Dear) so much,
    Lov'd I not Honour more.

Richard Lovelace

The Destruction of Sennacherib

The Assyrian came down like the wolf on the fold,
And his cohorts were gleaming in purple and gold;
And the sheen of their spears was like stars on the sea,
When the blue wave rolls nightly on deep Galilee.

Like the leaves of the forest when Summer is green,
That host with their banners at sunset were seen:
Like the leaves of the forest when Autumn hath blown,
That host on the morrow lay withered and strown.

For the Angel of Death spread his wings on the blast,
And breathed in the face of the foe as he passed;
And the eyes of the sleepers waxed deadly and chill,
And their hearts but once heaved, and for ever grew still!

And there lay the steed with his nostril all wide,
But through it there rolled not the breath of his pride;
And the foam of his gasping lay white on the turf,
And cold as the spray of the rock-beating surf.

And there lay the rider distorted and pale,
With the dew on his brow, and the rust on his mail:
And the tents were all silent, the banners alone,
The lances unlifted, the trumpet unblown.

And the widows of Ashur are loud in their wail,
And the idols are broke in the temple of Baal;
And the might of the Gentile, unsmote by the sword,
Hath melted like snow in the glance of the Lord!

Lord Byron

Casabianca

The boy stood on the burning deck
Whence all but him had fled;
The flame that lit the battle's wreck
Shone round him o'er the dead.

Yet beautiful and bright he stood,
As born to rule the storm;
A creature of heroic blood,
A proud, though childlike form.

The flames rolled on – he would not go
Without his father's word;
That father, faint in death below,
His voice no longer heard.

He called aloud – 'Say, father, say,
If yet my task is done?'
He knew not that the chieftain lay
Unconscious of his son.

'Speak, father!' once again he cried,
'If I may yet be gone!'
And but the booming shots replied,
And fast the flames rolled on.

Upon his brow he felt their breath,
And in his waving hair,
And looked from that lone post of death
In still, yet brave despair.

And shouted but once more aloud,
'My father! must I stay?'
While o'er him fast, through sail and shroud,
The wreathing fires made way.

They wrapt the ship in splendour wild,
They caught the flag on high,
And streamed above the gallant child,
Like banners in the sky.

There came a burst of thunder sound –
The boy – oh! where was he?
Ask of the winds that far around
With fragments strewed the sea! –

With mast, and helm, and pennon fair
That well had borne their part –
But the noblest thing that perished there
Was that young, faithful heart.

Felicia Dorothea Hemans

The War Song of Dinas Vawr

The mountain sheep are sweeter,
But the valley sheep are fatter;
We therefore deemed it meeter
To carry off the latter.
We made an expedition;
We met a host, and quelled it;
We forced a strong position,
And killed the men who held it.

On Dyfed's richest valley,
Where herds of kine were browsing,
We made a mighty sally,
To furnish our carousing.
Fierce warriors rushed to meet us;
We met them, and o'erthrew them:
They struggled hard to beat us;
But we conquered them, and slew them.

As we drove our prize at leisure,
The king marched forth to catch us:
His rage surpassed all measure,
But his people could not match us.
He fled to his hall-pillars;
And, ere our force we led off,
Some sacked his house and cellars,
While others cut his head off.

We there, in strife bewild'ring,
Spilt blood enough to swim in:
We orphaned many children,
And widowed many women.
The eagles and the ravens

We glutted with our foemen;
The heroes and the cravens,
The spearmen and the bowmen.

We brought away from battle,
And much their land bemoaned them,
Two thousand head of cattle,
And the head of him who owned them:
Ednyfed, king of Dyfed,
His head was borne before us;
His wine and beasts supplied our feasts,
And his overthrow, our chorus.

Thomas Love Peacock

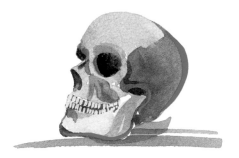

The Charge of the Light Brigade

I Half a league, half a league,
Half a league onward,
All in the valley of Death
    Rode the six hundred.
"Forward, the Light Brigade!
Charge for the guns!" he said.
Into the valley of Death
    Rode the six hundred.

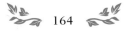

II   "Forward, the Light Brigade!"
    Was there a man dismayed?
    Not though the soldier knew
      Someone had blundered.
    Their's not to make reply,
    Their's not to reason why,
    Their's but to do and die.
    Into the valley of Death
      Rode the six hundred.

III   Cannon to right of them,
    Cannon to left of them,
    Cannon in front of them
      Volleyed and thundered;
    Stormed at with shot and shell,
    Boldly they rode and well,
    Into the jaws of Death,
    Into the mouth of hell
      Rode the six hundred.

IV   Flashed all their sabres bare,
    Flashed as they turned in air
    Sabring the gunners there,
    Charging an army, while
      All the world wondered.
    Plunged in the battery-smoke
    Right through the line they broke;
    Cossack and Russian
    Reeled from the sabre stroke
      Shattered and sundered.
    Then they rode back, but not
      Not the six hundred.

V   Cannon to right of them,
       Cannon to left of them,
       Cannon behind them
         Volleyed and thundered;
       Stormed at with shot and shell,
       While horse and hero fell.
       They that had fought so well
       Came through the jaws of Death,
       Back from the mouth of hell,
       All that was left of them,
         Left of six hundred.

VI   When can their glory fade?
       O the wild charge they made!
         All the world wondered.
       Honour the charge they made!
       Honour the Light Brigade,
         Noble six hundred!

Alfred, Lord Tennyson

O Captain! My Captain!

O Captain! my Captain! our fearful trip is done,
The ship has weather'd every rack, the prize we sought is won,
The port is near, the bells I hear, the people all exulting,
While follow eyes the steady keel, the vessel grim and daring;
   But O heart! heart! heart!
    O the bleeding drops of red,
     Where on the deck my Captain lies,
     Fallen cold and dead.

O Captain! my Captain! rise up and hear the bells;
Rise up—for you the flag is flung—for you the bugle trills,
For you bouquets and ribbon'd wreaths—for you the shores
 a-crowding,
For you they call, the swaying mass, their eager faces turning;
   Here Captain! dear father!
    This arm beneath your head!
     It is some dream that on the deck,
     You've fallen cold and dead.

My Captain does not answer, his lips are pale and still,
My father does not feel my arm, he has no pulse nor will,
The ship is anchor'd safe and sound, its voyage closed and
 done,
From fearful trip the victor ship comes in with object won;
   Exult O shores, and ring O bells!
    But I with mournful tread,
     Walk the deck my Captain lies,
     Fallen cold and dead.

Walt Whitman

Shiloh: A Requiem

Skimming lightly, wheeling still,
  The swallows fly low
Over the field in clouded days,
  The forest-field of Shiloh—
Over the field where April rain
Solaced the parched ones stretched in pain
Through the pause of night
That followed the Sunday fight
  Around the church of Shiloh—
The church so lone, the log-built one,
That echoed to many a parting groan
    And natural prayer
  Of dying foemen mingled there—
Foemen at morn, but friends at eve—
  Fame or country least their care:
(What like a bullet can undeceive!)
  But now they lie low,
While over them the swallows skim,
  And all is hushed at Shiloh.

Herman Melville

My Boy Jack

"Have you news of my boy Jack?"
Not this tide.
"When d'you think that he'll come back?"
Not with this wind blowing, and this tide.

"Has any one else had word of him?"
Not this tide.
For what is sunk will hardly swim,
Not with this wind blowing, and this tide.

"Oh, dear, what comfort can I find?"
None this tide,
Nor any tide,
Except he did not shame his kind —
Not even with that wind blowing, and that tide.

Then hold your head up all the more,
This tide,
And every tide;
Because he was the son you bore,
And gave to that wind blowing and that tide!

Rudyard Kipling

Drummer Hodge

They throw in Drummer Hodge, to rest
Uncoffined – just as found:
His landmark is a kopje-crest
That breaks the veldt around:
And foreign constellations west
Each night above his mound.

Young Hodge the drummer never knew –
Fresh from his Wessex home –
The meaning of the broad Karoo,
The Bush, the dusty loam,
And why uprose to nightly view
Strange stars amid the gloam.

Yet portion of that unknown plain
Will Hodge for ever be;
His homely Northern breast and brain
Grow to some Southern tree,
And strange-eyed constellations reign
His stars eternally.

Thomas Hardy

War is Kind

Do not weep, maiden, for war is kind,
Because your lover threw wild hands toward the sky
And the affrighted steed ran on alone,
Do not weep.
War is kind.

Hoarse, booming drums of the regiment,
Little souls who thirst for fight,
These men were born to drill and die.
The unexplained glory flies above them.
Great is the battle-god, great, and his kingdom—
A field where a thousand corpses lie.

Do not weep, babe, for war is kind.
Because your father tumbles in the yellow trenches,
Raged at his breast, gulped and died,
Do not weep.
War is kind.

Swift blazing flag of the regiment,
Eagle with crest of red and gold,
These men were born to drill and die.
Point for them the virtue of slaughter,
Make plain to them the excellence of killing
And a field where a thousand corpses lie.

Mother whose heart hung humble as a button
On the bright splendid shroud of your son,
Do not weep.
War is kind!

Stephen Crane

'Here dead we lie'

Here dead we lie
Because we did not choose
To live and shame the land
From which we sprung.

Life, to be sure,
Is nothing much to lose,
But young men think it is,
And we were young.

A. E. Housman

172

The Soldier

If I should die, think only this of me:
  That there's some corner of a foreign field
That is forever England. There shall be
  In that rich earth a richer dust concealed;
A dust whom England bore, shaped, made aware,
  Gave, once, her flowers to love, her ways to roam,
A body of England's, breathing English air,
  Washed by the rivers, blest by the suns of home.

And think, this heart, all evil shed away,
  A pulse in the eternal mind, no less
    Gives somewhere back the thoughts by England given;
Her sights and sounds; dreams happy as her day;
  And laughter, learnt of friends; and gentleness,
    In hearts at peace, under an English heaven.

Rupert Brooke

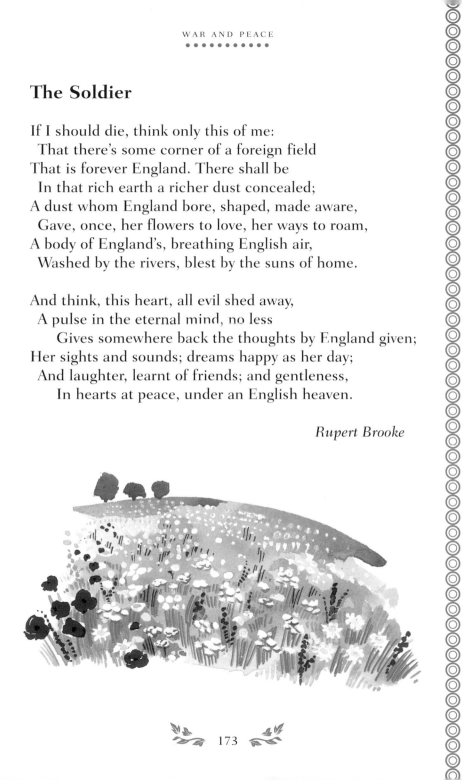

Anthem for Doomed Youth

What passing-bells for these who die as cattle?
Only the monstrous anger of the guns.
Only the stuttering rifles' rapid rattle
Can patter out their hasty orisons.
No mockeries now for them; no prayers nor bells;
Nor any voice of mourning save the choirs, –
The shrill, demented choirs of wailing shells;
And bugles calling for them from sad shires.
What candles may be held to speed them all?
Not in the hands of boys but in their eyes
Shall shine the holy glimmers of goodbyes.
The pallor of girls' brows shall be their pall;
Their flowers the tenderness of patient minds,
And each slow dusk a drawing-down of blinds.

Wilfred Owen

The Cherry Trees

The cherry trees bend over and are shedding,
On the old road where all that passed are dead,
Their petals, strewing the grass as for a wedding
This early May morn when there is none to wed.

Edward Thomas

In Flanders Fields

In Flanders fields the poppies blow
Between the crosses, row on row,
That mark our place; and in the sky
The larks, still bravely singing, fly
Scarce heard amid the guns below.

We are the Dead. Short days ago
We lived, felt dawn, saw sunset glow,
Loved and were loved, and now we lie
In Flanders fields.

Take up our quarrel with the foe:
To you from failing hands we throw
The torch; be yours to hold it high.
If ye break faith with us who die
We shall not sleep, though poppies grow
In Flanders fields.

John McCrae

Peace

Now, God be thanked Who has matched us with His hour,
And caught our youth, and wakened us from sleeping,
With hand made sure, clear eye, and sharpened power,
To turn, as swimmers into cleanness leaping,
Glad from a world grown old and cold and weary,
Leave the sick hearts that honour could not move,
And half-men, and their dirty songs and dreary,
And all the little emptiness of love!

Oh! we, who have known shame, we have found release there,
Where there's no ill, no grief, but sleep has mending,
Naught broken save this body, lost but breath;
Nothing to shake the laughing heart's long peace there
But only agony, and that has ending;
And the worst friend and enemy is but Death.

Rupert Brooke

Everyone Sang

Everyone suddenly burst out singing;
And I was filled with such delight
As prisoned birds must find in freedom,
Winging wildly across the white
Orchards and dark-green fields; on–on–and out of sight.
Everyone's voice was suddenly lifted;
And beauty came like the setting sun:
My heart was shaken with tears; and horror
Drifted away ... O, but Everyone
Was a bird; and the song was wordless;
   the singing will never be done.

Siegfried Sassoon

176

Mortality
and Remembrance

'Methought I saw my late espoused saint'

Methought I saw my late espoused saint
    Brought to me, like Alcestis, from the grave,
    Whom Jove's great son to her glad husband gave,
    Rescu'd from death by force, though pale and faint.
Mine, as whom wash'd from spot of child-bed taint
    Purification in the old Law did save,
    And such as yet once more I trust to have
    Full sight of her in Heaven without restraint,
Came vested all in white, pure as her mind;
    Her face was veil'd, yet to my fancied sight
    Love, sweetness, goodness, in her person shin'd
So clear as in no face with more delight.
    But Oh! as to embrace me she inclin'd,
    I wak'd, she fled, and day brought back my night.

John Milton

Little Boy Blue

The little toy dog is covered with dust,
    But sturdy and staunch he stands;
The little toy soldier is red with rust,
    And his musket moulds in his hands.
Time was when the little toy dog was new,
    And the soldier was passing fair;
And that was the time when our Little Boy Blue
    Kissed them and put them there.

'Now don't you go till I come,' he said,
    'And don't you make any noise!'
So, toddling off to his trundle bed,
    He dreamt of the pretty toys;

And, as he was dreaming, an angel song
    Awakened our Little Boy Blue—
Oh! the years are many, the years are long,
    But the little toy friends are true!

Ay, faithful to Little Boy Blue they stand,
    Each in the same old place,
Awaiting the touch of a little hand,
    The smile of a little face;
And they wonder, as waiting the long years through
    In the dust of that little chair,
What has become of our Little Boy Blue,
    Since he kissed them and put them there.

Eugene Field

Sonnet 55 'Not marble, nor the gilded monuments'

Not marble, nor the gilded monuments
Of princes, shall outlive this powerful rhyme;
But you shall shine more bright in these contents
Than unswept stone, besmear'd with sluttish time.
When wasteful war shall statues overturn,
And broils root out the work of masonry,
Nor Mars his sword nor war's quick fire shall burn
The living record of your memory.
'Gainst death and all-oblivious enmity
Shall you pace forth; your praise shall still find room
Even in the eyes of all posterity
That wear this world out to the ending doom.
So, till the judgment that yourself arise,
You live in this, and dwell in lovers' eyes.

William Shakespeare

'They are all gone into the world of light!'

They are all gone into the world of light!
    And I alone sit ling'ring here;
Their very memory is fair and bright,
    And my sad thoughts doth clear.

It glows and glitters in my cloudy breast,
    Like stars upon some gloomy grove,
Or those faint beams in which this hill is drest,
    After the sun's remove.

I see them walking in an air of glory,
    Whose light doth trample on my days:
My days, which are at best but dull and hoary,
    Mere glimmering and decays.

O holy Hope! and high Humility,
    High as the heavens above!
These are your walks, and you have show'd them me
    To kindle my cold love.

Dear, beauteous Death! the jewel of the just,
    Shining nowhere, but in the dark;
What mysteries do lie beyond thy dust
    Could man outlook that mark!

He that hath found some fledg'd bird's nest, may know
    At first sight, if the bird be flown;
But what fair well or grove he sings in now,
    That is to him unknown.

And yet as angels in some brighter dreams
 Call to the soul, when man doth sleep:
So some strange thoughts transcend our wonted themes
 And into glory peep.

If a star were confin'd into a tomb,
 Her captive flames must needs burn there;
But when the hand that lock'd her up, gives room,
 She'll shine through all the sphere.

O Father of eternal life, and all
 Created glories under thee!
Resume thy spirit from this world of thrall
 Into true liberty.

Either disperse these mists, which blot and fill
 My perspective still as they pass,
Or else remove me hence unto that hill,
 Where I shall need no glass.

Henry Vaughan

Extract from 'In Memoriam', Canto 27

I envy not in any moods
    The captive void of noble rage,
    The linnet born within the cage,
That never knew the summer woods:

I envy not the beast that takes
    His license in the field of time,
    Unfetter'd by the sense of crime,
To whom a conscience never wakes;

Nor, what may count itself as blest,
    The heart that never plighted troth
    But stagnates in the weeds of sloth;
Nor any want-begotten rest.

I hold it true, whate'er befall;
    I feel it, when I sorrow most;
    'Tis better to have loved and lost
Than never to have loved at all.

Alfred, Lord Tennyson

Virtue

Sweet day, so cool, so calm, so bright,
The bridal of the earth and sky;
The dew shall weep thy fall to-night,
        For thou must die.

Sweet rose, whose hue angry and brave
Bids the rash gazer wipe his eye;
Thy root is ever in its grave,
        And thou must die.

Sweet spring, full of sweet days and roses,
A box where sweets compacted lie;
My music shows ye have your closes,
        And all must die.

Only a sweet and virtuous soul,
Like season'd timber, never gives;
But though the whole world turn to coal,
        Then chiefly lives.

George Herbert

Requiescat

Strew on her roses, roses,
    And never a spray of yew!
In quiet she reposes;
    Ah, would that I did too!

Her mirth the world required;
    She bathed it in smiles of glee.
But her heart was tired, tired,
    And now they let her be.

Her life was turning, turning,
    In mazes of heat and sound.
But for peace her soul was yearning,
    And now peace laps her round.

Her cabin'd, ample spirit,
    It flutter'd and fail'd for breath.
To-night it doth inherit
    The vasty hall of death.

Matthew Arnold

Remember

Remember me when I am gone away,
    Gone far away into the silent land;
    When you can no more hold me by the hand,
Nor I half turn to go yet turning stay.
Remember me when no more day by day
    You tell me of our future that you plann'd:
    Only remember me; you understand

184

It will be late to counsel then or pray.
Yet if you should forget me for a while
    And afterwards remember, do not grieve:
    For if the darkness and corruption leave
    A vestige of the thoughts that once I had,
Better by far you should forget and smile
    Than that you should remember and be sad.

Christina Rossetti

'After great pain, a formal feeling comes'

After great pain, a formal feeling comes –
The Nerves sit ceremonious, like Tombs –
The stiff Heart questions 'was it He, that bore,'
And 'Yesterday, or Centuries before'?

The Feet, mechanical, go round –
A Wooden way
Of Ground, or Air, or Ought –
Regardless grown,
A Quartz contentment, like a stone –

This is the Hour of Lead –
Remembered, if outlived,
As Freezing persons, recollect the Snow –
First – Chill – then Stupor – then the letting go –

Emily Dickinson

Transformations

Portion of this yew
Is a man my grandsire knew,
Bosomed here at its foot:
This branch may be his wife,
A ruddy human life
Now turned to a green shoot.

These grasses must be made
Of her who often prayed,
Last century, for repose;
And the fair girl long ago
Whom I often tried to know
May be entering this rose.

So, they are not underground,
But as nerves and veins abound
In the growths of upper air,
And they feel the sun and rain,
And the energy again
That made them what they were!

Thomas Hardy

The Old Familiar Faces

I have had playmates, I have had companions,
In my days of childhood, in my joyful school-days,
All, all are gone, the old familiar faces.

I have been laughing, I have been carousing,
Drinking late, sitting late, with my bosom cronies,
All, all are gone, the old familiar faces.

I loved a love once, fairest among women;
Closed are her doors on me, I must not see her —
All, all are gone, the old familiar faces.

I have a friend, a kinder friend has no man;
Like an ingrate, I left my friend abruptly;
Left him, to muse on the old familiar faces.

Ghost-like, I paced round the haunts of my childhood.
Earth seemed a desert I was bound to traverse,
Seeking to find the old familiar faces.

Friend of my bosom, thou more than a brother,
Why wert not thou born in my father's dwelling?
So might we talk of the old familiar faces —

How some they have died, and some they have left me,
And some are taken from me; all are departed;
All, all are gone, the old familiar faces.

Charles Lamb

Surprised by Joy

Surprised by joy—impatient as the Wind
I turned to share the transport—Oh! with whom
But Thee, long buried in the silent Tomb,
That spot which no vicissitude can find?
Love, faithful love, recalled thee to my mind—
But how could I forget thee?—Through what power,
Even for the least division of an hour,
Have I been so beguiled as to be blind
To my most grievous loss!—That thought's return
Was the worst pang that sorrow ever bore,
Save one, one only, when I stood forlorn,
Knowing my heart's best treasure was no more;
That neither present time, nor years unborn
Could to my sight that heavenly face restore.

William Wordsworth

Grief

I tell you, hopeless grief is passionless;
That only men incredulous of despair,
Half-taught in anguish, through the midnight air
Beat upward to God's throne in loud access
Of shrieking and reproach. Full desertness,
In souls as countries, lieth silent-bare
Under the blanching, vertical eye-glare
Of the absolute heavens. Deep-hearted man, express
Grief for thy dead in silence like to death—
Most like a monumental statue set
In everlasting watch and moveless woe
Till itself crumble to the dust beneath.
Touch it; the marble eyelids are not wet:
If it could weep, it could arise and go.

Elizabeth Barrett Browning

On His Seventy-Fifth Birthday

I strove with none; for none was worth my strife,
    Nature I loved, and next to Nature, Art;
I warmed both hands before the fire of life,
    It sinks, and I am ready to depart.

Walter Savage Landor

Requiem

Under the wide and starry sky,
Dig the grave and let me lie.
Glad did I live and gladly die,
    And I laid me down with a will.

This be the verse you grave for me:
Here he lies where he longed to be;
Home is the sailor, home from sea,
    And the hunter home from the hill.

Robert Louis Stevenson

No Worst There Is None

No worst, there is none. Pitched past pitch of grief,
More pangs will, schooled at forepangs, wilder wring.
Comforter, where, where is your comforting?
Mary, mother of us, where is your relief?
My cries heave, herds-long; huddle in a main, a chief
Woe, wórld-sorrow; on an áge-old anvil wince and sing —
Then lull, then leave off. Fury had shrieked 'No ling-
ering! Let me be fell: force I must be brief.'

    O the mind, mind has mountains; cliffs of fall
Frightful, sheer, no-man-fathomed. Hold them cheap
May who ne'er hung there. Nor does long our small
Durance deal with that steep or deep. Here! creep,
Wretch, under a comfort serves in a whirlwind: all
Life death does end and each day dies with sleep.

Gerard Manley Hopkins

190

Futility

Move him into the sun—
Gently its touch awoke him once,
At home, whispering of fields unsown.
Always it awoke him, even in France,
Until this morning and this snow.
If anything might rouse him now
The kind old sun will know.
Think how it wakes the seeds—
Woke, once, the clays of a cold star.
Are limbs so dear-achieved, are sides
Full-nerved,—still warm,—too hard to stir?
Was it for this the clay grew tall? —
O what made fatuous sunbeams toil
To break earth's sleep at all?

Wilfred Owen

'Do not stand at my grave and weep'

Do not stand at my grave and weep,
I am not there – I do not sleep.
I am the thousand winds that blow,
I am the diamond glints in snow,
I am the sunlight on ripened grain,
I am the gentle autumn rain.
As you awake with morning's hush
I am the swift-up-flinging rush
Of quiet birds in circling flight.
Do not stand at my grave and cry,
I am not there – I did not die.

Attributed to Mary Elizabeth Frye

Ballads and
Folk Poems

The Corpus Christi Carol

He bore him up, he bore him down,
He bore him into an orchard brown.
Lully, lullay, lully, lullay!
The falcon has borne my mate away.

In that orchard there was a hall
That was hanged with purple and pall;
Lully, lullay, lully, lullay!
The falcon has borne my mate away.

And in that hall there was a bed:
It was hanged with gold so red;
Lully, lullay, lully, lullay!
The falcon has borne my mate away.

And in that bed there lies a knight,
His wounds bleeding day and night;
Lully, lullay, lully, lullay!
The falcon has borne my mate away.

By that bed's side there kneels a maid,
And she weeps both night and day;
Lully, lullay, lully, lullay!
The falcon has borne my mate away.

And by that bed's side there stands a stone,
"The Body of Christ" written thereon.
Lully, lullay, lully, lullay!
The falcon has borne my mate away.

Anon, 15th century

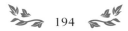

La Belle Dame Sans Merci

O what can ail thee, knight-at-arms,
    Alone and palely loitering?
The sedge has wither'd from the lake,
    And no birds sing.

O what can ail thee, knight-at-arms!
    So haggard and so woe-begone?
The squirrel's granary is full,
    And the harvest's done.

I see a lily on thy brow
    With anguish moist and fever dew,
And on thy cheeks a fading rose
    Fast withereth too.

I met a lady in the meads,
    Full beautiful—a faery's child,
Her hair was long, her foot was light,
    And her eyes were wild.

I made a garland for her head,
    And bracelets too, and fragrant zone;
She look'd at me as she did love,
    And made sweet moan.

I set her on my pacing steed,
    And nothing else saw all day long,
For sidelong would she bend, and sing
    A faery's song.

She found me roots of relish sweet,
    And honey wild, and manna dew,
And sure in language strange she said—
    'I love thee true.'

She took me to her elfin grot,
    And there she wept, and sigh'd fill sore,
And there I shut her wild wild eyes
    With kisses four.

And there she lulled me asleep,
    And there I dream'd—Ah! woe betide!
The latest dream I ever dream'd
    On the cold hill's side.

I saw pale kings and princes too,
    Pale warriors, death-pale were they all;
They cried—'La Belle Dame sans Merci
    Hath thee in thrall!'

I saw their starved lips in the gloam,
    With horrid warning gaped wide,
And I awoke and found me here,
    On the cold hill's side.

And this is why I sojourn here,
    Alone and palely loitering,
Though the sedge is wither'd from the lake,
    And no birds sing.

John Keats

Comin' Thro' the Rye

Comin thro' the rye, poor body,
Comin thro' the rye,
She draigl't a' her petticoatie
Comin thro' the rye.

Oh Jenny's a' weet, poor body,
Jenny's seldom dry,
She draigl't a' her petticoatie
Comin thro' the rye.

Gin a body meet a body
Comin thro' the rye,
Gin a body kiss a body
Need a body cry.

Gin a body meet a body
Comin thro' the glen;
Gin a body kiss a body
Need the warld ken!

Oh Jenny's a' weet, poor body,
Jenny's seldom dry,
She draigl't a' her petticoatie
Comin thro' the rye.

Robert Burns

Ballad: It Was the Time of Roses

It was not in the winter
    Our loving lot was cast!
It was the time of roses,
    We plucked them as we passed!

That churlish season never frowned
    On early lovers yet! –
Oh no – the world was newly crowned
    With flowers, when first we met.

'Twas twilight, and I bade you go,
    But still you held me fast; –
It was the time of roses, –
    We plucked them as we passed!

What else could peer my glowing cheek
    That tears began to stud? –
And when I asked the like of Love
    You snatched a damask bud, –

And oped it to the dainty core
    Still glowing to the last: –
It was the time of roses,
    We plucked them as we passed!

Thomas Hood

Lochinvar

O young Lochinvar is come out of the west,
Through all the wide Border his steed was the best;
And save his good broadsword he weapons had none,
He rode all unarm'd, and he rode all alone.
So faithful in love, and so dauntless in war,
There never was knight like the young Lochinvar.

He staid not for brake, and he stopp'd not for stone,
He swam the Eske river where ford there was none;
But ere he alighted at Netherby gate,
The bride had consented, the gallant came late:
For a laggard in love, and a dastard in war,
Was to wed the fair Ellen of brave Lochinvar.

So boldly he enter'd the Netherby Hall,
Among bride's-men, and kinsmen, and brothers and all:
Then spoke the bride's father, his hand on his sword,
(For the poor craven bridegroom said never a word,)
'O come ye in peace here, or come ye in war,
Or to dance at our bridal, young Lord Lochinvar?'

'I long woo'd your daughter, my suit you denied;—
Love swells like the Solway, but ebbs like its tide—
And now I am come, with this lost love of mine,
To lead but one measure, drink one cup of wine.
There are maidens in Scotland more lovely by far,
That would gladly be bride to the young Lochinvar.'

The bride kiss'd the goblet: the knight took it up,
He quaff'd off the wine, and he threw down the cup.
She look'd down to blush, and she look'd up to sigh,
With a smile on her lips and a tear in her eye.
He took her soft hand, ere her mother could bar,—
'Now tread we a measure!' said young Lochinvar.

So stately his form, and so lovely her face,
That never a hall such a galliard did grace;
While her mother did fret, and her father did fume,
And the bridegroom stood dangling his bonnet and plume;
And the bride-maidens whisper'd, ''twere better by far
To have match'd our fair cousin with young Lochinvar.'

One touch to her hand, and one word in her ear,
When they reach'd the hall-door, and the charger stood near;
So light to the croupe the fair lady he swung,
So light to the saddle before her he sprung!
'She is won! we are gone, over bank, bush, and scaur;
They'll have fleet steeds that follow,' quoth young Lochinvar.

There was mounting 'mong Graemes of the Netherby clan;
Forsters, Fenwicks, and Musgraves, they rode and they ran:
There was racing and chasing on Cannobie Lee,
But the lost bride of Netherby ne'er did they see.
So daring in love, and so dauntless in war,
Have ye e'er heard of gallant like young Lochinvar?

Walter Scott

Scarborough Fair

Are you going to Scarborough Fair?
Parsley, sage, rosemary, and thyme;
Remember me to the one who lives there,
For once she was a true love of mine.

Tell her to make me a cambric shirt,
Parsley, sage, rosemary, and thyme;
Sewn without seams or fine needlework,
If she would be a true love of mine.

Tell her to wash it in yonder well,
Parsley, sage, rosemary, and thyme;
Where never spring water or rain ever fell,
And she shall be a true love of mine.

Tell her to dry it on yonder thorn,
Parsley, sage, rosemary, and thyme;
Which never bore blossom since Adam was born,
Then she shall be a true love of mine.

Now he has asked me questions three,
Parsley, sage, rosemary, and thyme;
I hope he'll answer as many for me
Before he shall be a true love of mine.

Tell him to buy me an acre of land,
Parsley, sage, rosemary, and thyme;
Between the salt water and the sea sand,
Then he shall be a true love of mine.

Tell him to plough it with a ram's horn,
Parsley, sage, rosemary, and thyme;
And sow it all over with one pepper corn,
And he shall be a true love of mine.

Tell him to sheer't with a sickle of leather,
Parsley, sage, rosemary, and thyme;
And bind it up with a peacock feather.
And he shall be a true love of mine.

Tell him to thrash it on yonder wall,
Parsley, sage, rosemary, and thyme,
And never let one corn of it fall,
Then he shall be a true love of mine.

When he has done and finished his work.
Parsley, sage, rosemary, and thyme:
Oh, tell him to come and he'll have his shirt,
And he shall be a true love of mine.

Anonymous

Barbara Frietchie

Up from the meadows rich with corn,
Clear in the cool September morn,

The clustered spires of Frederick stand
Green-walled by the hills of Maryland.

Round about them orchards sweep,
Apple- and peach-tree fruited deep,

Fair as a garden of the Lord
To the eyes of the famished rebel horde,

On that pleasant morn of the early fall
When Lee marched over the mountain wall,—

Over the mountains winding down,
Horse and foot, into Frederick town.

Forty flags with their silver stars,
Forty flags with their crimson bars,

Flapped in the morning wind: the sun
Of noon looked down, and saw not one.

Up rose old Barbara Frietchie then,
Bowed with her fourscore years and ten;

Bravest of all in Frederick town,
She took up the flag the men hauled down;

In her attic window the staff she set,
To show that one heart was loyal yet.

Up the street came the rebel tread,
Stonewall Jackson riding ahead.

Under his slouched hat left and right
He glanced: the old flag met his sight.

'Halt!'— the dust-brown ranks stood fast.
'Fire!'— out blazed the rifle-blast.

It shivered the window, pane and sash;
It rent the banner with seam and gash.

Quick, as it fell, from the broken staff
Dame Barbara snatched the silken scarf;

She leaned far out on the window-sill,
And shook it forth with a royal will.

'Shoot, if you must, this old gray head,
But spare your country's flag,' she said.

A shade of sadness, a blush of shame,
Over the face of the leader came;

The nobler nature within him stirred
To life at that woman's deed and word:

'Who touches a hair of yon gray head
Dies like a dog! March on!' he said.

All day long through Frederick street
Sounded the tread of marching feet:

All day long that free flag tost
Over the heads of the rebel host.

Ever its torn folds rose and fell
On the loyal winds that loved it well;

And through the hill-gaps sunset light
Shone over it with a warm good-night.

Barbara Frietchie's work is o'er,
And the Rebel rides on his raids no more.

Honor to her! and let a tear
Fall, for her sake, on Stonewall's bier.

Over Barbara Frietchie's grave
Flag of Freedom and Union, wave!

Peace and order and beauty draw
Round thy symbol of light and law;

And ever the stars above look down
On thy stars below in Frederick town!

John Greenleaf Whittier

Big Steamers

'Oh, where are you going to, all you Big Steamers,
  With England's own coal, up and down the salt seas?'
'We are going to fetch you your bread and your butter,
  Your beef, pork, and mutton, eggs, apples, and cheese.'

'And where will you fetch it from, all you Big Steamers,
  And where shall I write you when you are away?'
'We fetch it from Melbourne, Quebec, and Vancouver–
  Address us at Hobart, Hong-Kong, and Bombay.'

'But if anything happened to all you Big Steamers,
  And suppose you were wrecked up and down the salt sea?'
'Then you'd have no coffee or bacon for breakfast,
  And you'd have no muffins or toast for your tea.'

'Then I'll pray for fine weather for all you Big Steamers,
  For little blue billows and breezes so soft.'
'Oh, billows and breezes don't bother Big Steamers,
  For we're iron below and steel-rigging aloft.'

'Then I'll build a new lighthouse for all you Big Steamers,
  With plenty wise pilots to pilot you through.'
'Oh, the Channel's as bright as a ball-room already,
  And pilots are thicker than pilchards at Looe.'

'Then what can I do for you, all you Big Steamers,
  Oh, what can I do for your comfort and good?'
'Send out your big warships to watch your big waters,
  That no one may stop us from bringing you food.'

'For the bread that you eat and the biscuits you nibble,
  The sweets that you suck and the joints that you carve,
They are brought to you daily by all us Big Steamers–
  And if one hinders our coming you'll starve!'

Rudyard Kipling

The Lady of Shalott

PART I

On either side the river lie
Long fields of barley and of rye,
That clothe the wold and meet the sky;
And thro' the field the road runs by
      To many-tower'd Camelot;
And up and down the people go,
Gazing where the lilies blow
Round an island there below,
      The island of Shalott.

Willows whiten, aspens quiver,
Little breezes dusk and shiver
Thro' the wave that runs for ever
By the island in the river
      Flowing down to Camelot.
Four gray walls, and four gray towers,
Overlook a space of flowers,
And the silent isle imbowers
      The Lady of Shalott.

By the margin, willow-veil'd,
Slide the heavy barges trail'd
By slow horses; and unhail'd
The shallop flitteth silken-sail'd
      Skimming down to Camelot:
But who hath seen her wave her hand?
Or at the casement seen her stand?
Or is she known in all the land,
      The Lady of Shalott?

Only reapers, reaping early
In among the bearded barley,
Hear a song that echoes cheerly
From the river winding clearly,
    Down to tower'd Camelot:
And by the moon the reaper weary,
Piling sheaves in uplands airy,
Listening, whispers ''Tis the fairy
    Lady of Shalott.'

PART II

There she weaves by night and day
A magic web with colours gay.
She has heard a whisper say,
A curse is on her if she stay
    To look down to Camelot.
She knows not what the curse may be,
And so she weaveth steadily,
And little other care hath she,
    The Lady of Shalott.

And moving thro' a mirror clear
That hangs before her all the year,
Shadows of the world appear.
There she sees the highway near
    Winding down to Camelot:
There the river eddy whirls,
And there the surly village-churls,
And the red cloaks of market girls,
    Pass onward from Shalott.

Sometimes a troop of damsels glad,
An abbot on an ambling pad,
Sometimes a curly shepherd-lad,
Or long-hair'd page in crimson clad,
    Goes by to tower'd Camelot;
And sometimes thro' the mirror blue
The knights come riding two and two:
She hath no loyal knight and true,
    The Lady of Shalott.

But in her web she still delights
To weave the mirror's magic sights,
For often thro' the silent nights
A funeral, with plumes and lights,
    And music, went to Camelot:
Or when the moon was overhead,
Came two young lovers lately wed;
'I am half sick of shadows,' said
    The Lady of Shalott.

PART III

A bow-shot from her bower-eaves,
He rode between the barley-sheaves,
The sun came dazzling thro' the leaves,
And flamed upon the brazen greaves
     Of bold Sir Lancelot.
A red-cross knight for ever kneel'd
To a lady in his shield,
That sparkled on the yellow field,
     Beside remote Shalott.

The gemmy bridle glitter'd free,
Like to some branch of stars we see
Hung in the golden Galaxy.
The bridle bells rang merrily
     As he rode down to Camelot:
And from his blazon'd baldric slung
A mighty silver bugle hung,
And as he rode his armour rung,
     Beside remote Shalott.

All in the blue unclouded weather
Thick-jewell'd shone the saddle-leather,
The helmet and the helmet-feather
Burn'd like one burning flame together,
     As he rode down to Camelot.
As often thro' the purple night,
Below the starry clusters bright,
Some bearded meteor, trailing light,
     Moves over still Shalott.

His broad clear brow in sunlight glow'd;
On burnish'd hooves his war-horse trode;
From underneath his helmet flow'd
His coal-black curls as on he rode,
     As he rode down to Camelot.
From the bank and from the river
He flash'd into the crystal mirror,
'Tirra lirra,' by the river
     Sang Sir Lancelot.

She left the web, she left the loom,
She made three paces thro' the room,
She saw the water-lily bloom,
She saw the helmet and the plume,
     She look'd down to Camelot.
Out flew the web and floated wide;
The mirror crack'd from side to side;
'The curse is come upon me!' cried
     The Lady of Shalott.

PART IV

In the stormy east-wind straining,
The pale yellow woods were waning,
The broad stream in his banks complaining,
Heavily the low sky raining
     Over tower'd Camelot;
Down she came and found a boat
Beneath a willow left afloat,
And round about the prow she wrote
     The Lady of Shalott.

And down the river's dim expanse—
Like some bold seer in a trance,
Seeing all his own mischance—
With a glassy countenance
     Did she look to Camelot.
And at the closing of the day
She loosed the chain, and down she lay;
The broad stream bore her far away,
     The Lady of Shalott.

Lying, robed in snowy white
That loosely flew to left and right—
The leaves upon her falling light—
Thro' the noises of the night
     She floated down to Camelot:
And as the boat-head wound along
The willowy hills and fields among,
They heard her singing her last song,
     The Lady of Shalott.

Heard a carol, mournful, holy,
Chanted loudly, chanted lowly,
Till her blood was frozen slowly,
And her eyes were darken'd wholly,
     Turn'd to tower'd Camelot;
For ere she reach'd upon the tide
The first house by the water-side,
Singing in her song she died,
     The Lady of Shalott.

Under tower and balcony,
By garden-wall and gallery,
A gleaming shape she floated by,
Dead-pale between the houses high,
    Silent into Camelot.
Out upon the wharfs they came,
Knight and burgher, lord and dame,
And round the prow they read her name,
    The Lady of Shalott.

Who is this? and what is here?
And in the lighted palace near
Died the sound of royal cheer;
And they cross'd themselves for fear,
    All the knights at Camelot:
But Lancelot mused a little space;
He said, 'She has a lovely face;
God in His mercy lend her grace,
    The Lady of Shalott.'

Alfred, Lord Tennyson

213

Maude Clare

Out of the church she followed them
With a lofty step and mien:
His bride was like a village maid,
Maude Clare was like a queen.

'Son Thomas,' his lady mother said,
With smiles, almost with tears:
'May Nell and you but live as true
As we have done for years;

'Your father thirty years ago
Had just your tale to tell;
But he was not so pale as you,
Nor I so pale as Nell.'

My lord was pale with inward strife,
And Nell was pale with pride;
My lord gazed long on pale Maude Clare
Or ever he kissed the bride.

'Lo, I have brought my gift, my lord,
Have brought my gift,' she said:
To bless the hearth, to bless the board,
To bless the marriage-bed.

'Here's my half of the golden chain
You wore about your neck,
That day we waded ankle-deep
For lilies in the beck:

'Here's my half of the faded leaves
We plucked from the budding bough,
With feet amongst the lily leaves, –
The lilies are budding now.'

He strove to match her scorn with scorn,
He faltered in his place:
'Lady,' he said, – 'Maude Clare,' he said, –
'Maude Clare,' – and hid his face.

She turn'd to Nell: 'My Lady Nell,
I have a gift for you;
Though, were it fruit, the blooms were gone,
Or, were it flowers, the dew.

'Take my share of a fickle heart,
Mine of a paltry love:
Take it or leave it as you will,
I wash my hands thereof.'

'And what you leave,' said Nell, 'I'll take,
And what you spurn, I'll wear;
For he's my lord for better and worse,
And him I love Maude Clare.

'Yea, though you're taller by the head,
More wise and much more fair:
I'll love him till he loves me best,
Me best of all Maude Clare.'

Christina Rossetti

Waltzing Matilda

Oh there once was a swagman camped in the billabongs,
  Under the shade of a Coolibah tree;
And he sang as he looked at the old billy boiling
  'Who'll come a-waltzing Matilda with me.'

Who'll come a-waltzing Matilda, my darling.
  Who'll come a-waltzing Matilda with me.
Waltzing Matilda and leading a water-bag.
  Who'll come a-waltzing Matilda with me.

Up came the jumbuck to drink at the waterhole,
  Up jumped the swagman and grabbed him with glee;
And he sang as he put him away in his tucker-bag,
  'Who'll come a-waltzing Matilda with me.'

Who'll come a-waltzing Matilda, my darling.
  Who'll come a-waltzing Matilda with me.
Waltzing Matilda and leading a water-bag.
  Who'll come a-waltzing Matilda with me.

Up came the squatter a-riding his thoroughbred;
  Up came the policeman – one, two, and three.
'Whose is the jumbuck you've got in the tucker-bag?
  You'll come a-waltzing Matilda with we.'

Who'll come a-waltzing Matilda, my darling.
  Who'll come a-waltzing Matilda with me.
Waltzing Matilda and leading a water-bag.
  Who'll come a-waltzing Matilda with me.

Up sprang the swagman and jumped into the waterhole,
  Drowning himself by the Coolibah tree;
And his voice can be heard as it sings in the billabongs,
  'Who'll come a-waltzing Matilda with me.'

Who'll come a-waltzing Matilda, my darling.
  Who'll come a-waltzing Matilda with me.
Waltzing Matilda and leading a water-bag.
  Who'll come a-waltzing Matilda with me.

Banjo Paterson

Three Fishers

Three fishers went sailing away to the west,
Away to the west as the sun went down;
Each thought on the woman who loved him the best,
And the children stood watching them out of the town;
For men must work, and women must weep,
And there's little to earn, and many to keep,
Though the harbour bar be moaning.

Three wives sat up in the lighthouse tower,
And they trimmed the lamps as the sun went down;
They looked at the squall, and they looked at the shower,
And the night-rack came rolling up ragged and brown.
But men must work, and women must weep,
Though storms be sudden, and waters deep,
And the harbour bar be moaning.

Three corpses lay out on the shining sands
In the morning gleam as the tide went down,
And the women are weeping and wringing their hands
For those who will never come home to the town;
For men must work, and women must weep,
And the sooner it's over, the sooner to sleep;
And good-bye to the bar and its moaning.

Charles Kingsley

The Ballad of Moll Magee

Come round me, little childer;
There, don't fling stones at me
Because I mutter as I go;
But pity Moll Magee.

My man was a poor fisher
With shore lines in the say;
My work was saltin' herrings
The whole of the long day.

And sometimes from the saltin' shed
I scarce could drag my feet,
Under the blessed moonlight,
Along the pebbly street.

I'd always been but weakly,
And my baby was just born;
A neighbour minded her by day,
I minded her till morn.

I lay upon my baby;
Ye little childer dear,
I looked on my cold baby
When the morn grew frosty and clear.

A weary woman sleeps so hard!
My man grew red and pale,
And gave me money, and bade me go
To my own place, Kinsale.

He drove me out and shut the door,
And gave his curse to me;
I went away in silence,
No neighbour could I see.

The windows and the doors were shut,
One star shone faint and green,
The little straws were turnin' round
Across the bare boreen.

I went away in silence;
Beyond old Martin's byre
I saw a kindly neighbour
Blowin' her mornin' fire.

She drew from me my story—
My money's all used up,
And still, with pityin', scornin' eye,
She gives me bite and sup.

She says my man will surely come
And fetch me home agin;
But always, as I'm movin' round,
Without doors or within,

Pilin' the wood or pilin' the turf,
Or goin' to the well,
I'm thinkin' of my baby
And keenin' to mysel'.

And sometimes I am sure she knows
When, openin' wide His door,
God lights the stars, His candles,
And looks upon the poor.

So now, ye little childer,
Ye won't fling stones at me;
But gather with your shinin' looks
And pity Moll Magee.

                                        W. B. Yeats

Author Index

Index of Titles and First Lines

Entries in *italics* are titles of poems.